MAGLIPAY
UNIVERSALIST

Also by Fredric John Muir:

Heretics' Faith: Vocabulary for Religious Liberals

A Reason for Hope: Liberation Theology Confronts a Liberal Church

Essays by the author found in:

Redeeming Time: Endowing Your Church with the Power of Covenant

With Purpose and Principle: Essays about the Seven Principles of Unitarian Universalism

Creating Safe Congregations: Toward an Ethic of Right Relations

MAGLIPAY UNIVERSALIST

The Unitarian Universalist Church of the Philippines

Fredric John Muir

Grateful acknowledgment is made for permission
to reprint "The Story of Toribio Quimada and
Universalism in the Philippines: A Church School
Curriculum," by Margaret K. Gooding and Rebecca
Quimada Sienes.

Maglipay Universalist: The Unitarian Universalist Church of the Philippines
© 2001 by Fredric John Muir

Library of Congress Card Number: 2001116226
ISBN 0-9707903-1-7

Cover design by James Santarelli

[Fear] is the single, most powerful constant among the people of this archipelago. We're raised to fear everything. Fate, gods, the elements of nature, authority, even joy.

—Ninotchka Rosca, *Twice Blessed*

To teach the hope that is for all, Proclaim the Universal call.

—Toribio S. Quimada, "Maglipay Universalist"

The Philippines

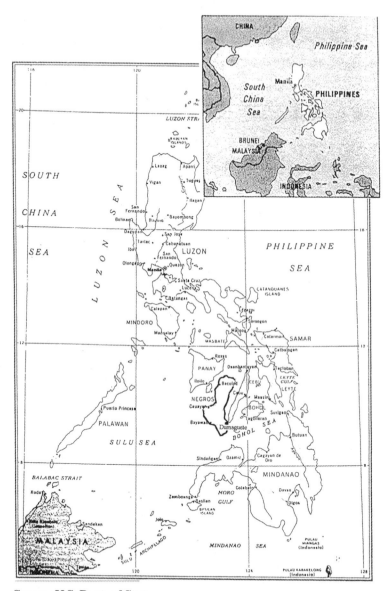

Source: U.S. Dept. of State.

Negros

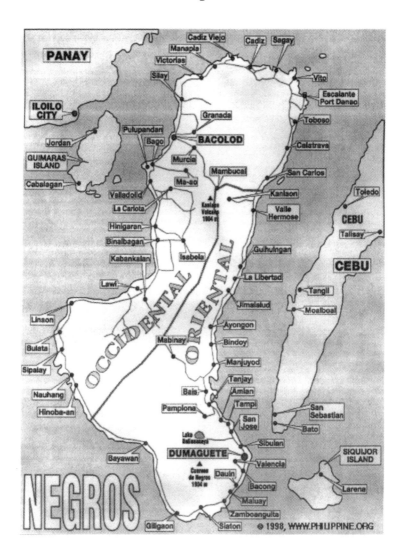

PANAY

ILOILO CITY

Cadiz Viejo
Manapla
Victorias
Silay
Cadiz
Sagay
Vito
Escalante
Port Danao
Toboso
Granada
Pulupandan
Jordan
Bago
BACOLOD
Calatrava
GUIMARAS ISLAND
Murcia
Mambucal
San Carlos
Cabalagan
Ma-ao
Kanlaon
Toledo
Valladolid
Kanlaon Volcano 1904 m
Valle Hermose
La Carlota
CEBU
Hinigaran
Talisay
Binalbagan
Isabela
Guihulngan
CEBU
Kabankalan
Lawi
La Libertad
Jimalalud
Tangil
Moalboal
Linaon
Ayongon
Bulata
Mabinay
Bindoy
Sipalay
Manjuyod
Nauhang
Tanjay
Hinoba-an
Bais
Amlan
Tampi
San Sebastian
Pamplona
San Jose
Bato
Lake Balinsasayo
Sibulan
SIQUIJOR ISLAND
Bayawan
DUMAGUETE
Valencia
Cuernos de Negros 1904 m
Dauin
Bacong
Larena
Maluay
Zamboanguita
Giligaon
Siaton
© 1998, WWW.PHILIPPINE.ORG

OCCIDENTAL

ORIENTAL

NEGROS

Contents

Acknowledgments   xi
Preface   xiii
1. A Short Introduction to the Philippines   1
2. Unitarianism in the Philippines   16
3. Universalism in the Philippines   24
4. Unitarian Universalism in the Philippines   42
5. Theology and the Unitarian Universalist Church
   of the Philippines   54
6. The Future of the Unitarian Universalist Church
   of the Philippines   73
Appendix 1. *Unitarians Face a New Age*, excerpt
   from the Commission of Appraisal
   of the American Unitarian
   Association, 1936   88
Appendix 2. The Biography of Rev. Toribio S.
   Quimada, by Melca Quimada Legaje   90
Appendix 3. The Constitution and Bylaws of the
   Unitarian Universalist Church of the
   Philippines   97
Appendix 4. Unitarian Universalist Congregations
   of the Philippines   136
Appendix 5. The Story of Toribio Quimada and
   Universalism in the Philippines: A
   Church School Curriculum, by
   Margaret K. Gooding and Rebecca
   Quimada Sienes   139
Sources   189

Acknowledgments

I wish to thank the Rev. Polly Guild and the International Council of Unitarian Universalists, and the Rev. William Murry, president of Meadville/Lombard Theological School, for their encouragement and aid. The Rev. Kenneth MacLean, special assistant to the president of the Unitarian Universalist Association for International Affairs, was determined to have me on the island of Negros and orchestrated the procurement of funds in a steady and sensitive manner; without his resourcefulness and commitment, my consultation, and hence this book, would not have been possible.

This project is funded in part by the Fund for International Unitarian Universalism. All proceeds from the sale of this book will be distributed to those serving the international Unitarian Universalist community, with the majority of the proceeds going to the Unitarian Universalist Church of the Philippines.

I am indebted to the Rev. Rebecca Q. Sienes, president of the Unitarian Universalist Church of the Philippines, for sharing with me her friendship, hospitality, and excellent historical research in two unpublished papers. She is a proud, strong, passionate, and inspiring Filipina.

Finally I wish to thank my home congregation, the Unitarian Universalist Church of Annapolis, Maryland, whose encouragement and support for this trip and project were never in question: they are one of our Association's outstanding congregations.

And then my wife, Karen. Eight years after my first visit to Negros in 1995, she wasn't too enthusiastic about my returning, but she knew that I was the right person for the job. Her support, understanding, and love saw me through some stressful and disappointing times—while abroad and during this project's completion. To experience this kind of unconditional support must be what grace is all about. I have been blessed.

Preface

My trip to Negros, Philippines, in 1991 was nearly accidental. I had just completed my doctor of ministry thesis at Wesley Theological Seminary in Washington, D.C. My sabbatical was but a month away and I wanted to go somewhere to "test out" my thesis, which was on liberation theology. Through a church connection, I had begun plans for a week in El Salvador followed by a week in Guatemala—in both cases, I would be talking liberation theology. My thesis advisor asked: "Isn't there a Unitarian Universalist context—somewhere in the world—where you could talk about liberation theology?" I shrugged—I didn't think so, I replied. He began naming countries starting in Central and South America. Eventually he named the Philippines. I had heard about Unitarian Universalism in the Philippines, but it was all pretty vague. I told him that I would have to look into it. He urged me to waste no time, and I didn't. The next day I called Unitarian Universalist Association headquarters and, yes, we did have congregations on one island, Negros—wherever that was!

What I knew about the Philippines, in general, could have been put into a short couple of sentences; what I knew about Unitarian Universalism on the island of Negros was even less. But within two months, I was flying to Manila, and then on to Dumaguete City—sight unseen—to spend two weeks that would blow my mind. Nothing could have prepared me for what I saw, what I would do, for the relationships that would become a part of my life.

Since then I have talked a lot about my experiences and what I have learned about Unitarian Universalism in a third-world context. As I have listened to questions and comments, I've learned, not surprisingly, that most people's knowledge of the Philippines is as limited as mine was: it's usually confined to the island of Luzon, specifically to one or two military bases and/or Manila. Many believe that the national language is Spanish and that Spanish customs prevail. Any sense of Philippine history—even American-Philippine history—is nil. Many struggle to find it on a world map. The Filipinos I worked and played with couldn't understand this, especially since their culture is permeated with American social, political, and cultural icons, standards, and assumptions.

So much that is written about the Philippines—by both Filipinos and others—whether scholarly works, tourist information, or general interest articles, gives scant acknowledgement to life outside Luzon (or maybe Mindanao). While the early Unitarian movement showed signs of life on Luzon and was based in Manila, my experiences have been only on Negros, just the opposite of the literature and journalism and the experiences of most Westerners. Compared to Luzon and Mindanao, Negros is tiny, and my travels on that island during the two months of my second visit were not as wide as I would have liked. Given these limits, I was often keenly aware during my writing of the temptation to make broad generalizations: "The Philippines," and "Filipinos," were two of the most tempting—as though I could speak with any degree of depth about the archipelago and all its residents. It was difficult enough to characterize those living on Negros! Still, there were times when such phrases seemed appropriate. Suffice it to say that this is not a book about the Philippines, but about Unitarian Universalism on Negros Island. Yet to understand the Unitarian Universalist Church of the Philippines, it still has been necessary to provide occasional background information—to portray with very broad strokes, the wider context.

Many of the experiences of my first visit were beginning to lose their crispness when eight years later the possibility arose for going back, this time for two months.

Though I was hesitant at first, by the time I arrived in Dumaguete City I knew that it was good and right, and I was impressed with how little had changed: a few more cars than eight years ago, a few more trucks, but the sounds of motorcabs, the smell of burning yard waste, the intensity of the sun, the blue of the sea, and the smiling faces and spirit of the people were all unchanged. This book is by no means intended to be the final word on Unitarian Universalism in the Philippines or on Negros. As I wrote, I became keenly aware of two reoccurring issues: First, that new sources and references will be forever emerging on this seemingly obscure topic. As the UUCP continues to grow and plays a more active role in the UUA and as Unitarian Universalism continues to flourish in regions outside the North Atlantic community, there will be more interest in the experiences of the UUCP, which will inevitably unearth further information. (The questions that follow each chapter are intended to promote discussion regarding the UUCP as well as the expanding international flavor of Unitarian Universalism.) And second, any new information will add to, and perhaps alter, what is presented in this small volume. This book is not intended to be an end, but a beginning. There is enough on the topic for many volumes to come, with far more detail. I can only hope that my research and work will have contributed to a strong start.

Finally, what Universalism brought to Negros (and to the Philippines) is amazing—its story, theology, and leadership are all amazing. Given Filipinos' history of oppression, fear, poverty, illiteracy, and isolation, the odds that this community of religious liberals proclaiming "Maglipay Universalist" ("Be joyful, Universalist") make for quite a story: the odds and circumstances have been poor for a faith of hope, equality, love, free thinking, and interdependence. But the odds and context appear to have been beaten: a new history is being written. Long live the Unitarian Universalist Church of the Philippines!

Chapter 1

A Short Introduction to the Philippines

The Philippines is like a broken rosary.

—Dumaguete City traffic officer

Waiting outside the bank in downtown Dumaguete City the traffic is heavy, the air is thick with the smell of diesel fuel, it is sunny, noisy, dusty, hot, and humid—it is a typical morning. Through the assortment of trucks, cars, bicycles, and even a couple of horse- and donkey-drawn carts, motorcabs are everywhere. Motorcabs are motorcycles with sidecars that are built to transport four passengers but often carry as many as six to eight and I've seen ten. While there appear to be no rules of the road for motorcabs, they keep moving about accident-free through the intersections. This morning they are being aided by a city traffic officer standing in the center of the lanes, though his directing efforts are barely detectable. When he spots me, he eases his way through the congestion and silently stands several feet away but still next to me. After a while he asks if I am an American. His questions follow a typical course: Where am I from? Where am I living? What am I doing on Negros? How long will I be staying? How do I like the Philippines? Eventually, he offers a comment: "They say the Philippines is like a broken rosary." This succinct statement about his native land is unique and insightful. More than a geolinguistic description, it portrays the archipelago's culture and history.

From north to south and spread out over 1,000 miles, the *Pilipinas* is 7,107 islands. A thousand of the islands are inhabited and fewer than five hundred are larger than a square mile. The Philippines is one of the world's largest archipelagoes, "one of nature's glories, a brilliant tapestry of land, sea and sky, fields, forest, mountains, wildlife and peoples—all so dazzling and diverse as to seem unreal." (Karnow 1989, 37) The archipelago is bordered on the north by Luzon and on the south by Mindanao, two islands that comprise almost two-thirds of the nation's land mass and that are home to a majority of Filipinos. Stanley Karnow (1989, 38), writes about this "quilt of contrasts": "Lush green plains and verdant hills stretch out against a horizon of jungle-clad peaks that soar as high as ten thousand feet, some active volcanoes. Placid lagoons enclosed by coral reefs bathe beaches of fine white sand, and elsewhere the surf dashes against rugged cliffs. With a coastline longer than that of the United States, everyplace is near the sea, itself a study in extremes. Shallow channels separate the islands, while the ocean off Mindanao plunges down six miles, the deepest spot on earth. Monsoon rains fall with biblical intensity, bringing fertility and decay."

There are eight languages of the Malayo-Polynesian family spoken in the Philippines, but only two languages are spoken with frequency: Tagalog (pronounced "tuh-GAH-log") and English. The national language is Tagalog, yet many do not speak it, especially outside of Luzon. While both Tagalog and English are taught in the schools and high school graduates are expected to be fluent in both, "More than half of all Filipinos speak English, and even when not doing so, drop English words into a patois nicknamed 'Taglish.'" (Kiester and Kiester 1999) Contrary to what many believe, Spanish is not the national language nor are you likely to hear it spoken anywhere (I met one man who said that his mother—a mestiza—occasionally spoke Spanish, but his father—of Chinese ancestry—discouraged it). Rather than Tagalog or English you are more likely to hear spoken a regional dialect—there are more than eighty! So profuse and common are the dialects that intranation communication can be burdensome. For example, a resident of Dumaguete City, where Cebuano is spoken, will not be able to speak with someone from Manila, where they speak Tagalog. Television and radio programs broadcast from Manila are in Tagalog and are not understood by those who speak another dialect. This hardship is even found on the same island where several dialects might be spoken. For example, Negros has two provinces: in Negros Oriental they speak Cebuano and in Negros Occidental the dialect is Hiligaynon. Communication between the provincial capitals, Dumaguete City and Bacolod, requires fluency in both dialects and/or Tagalog and/or English. I met an American doctor who described his first year, when he was learning the dialects of Negros Island. He said it was a comedy of errors since the same word, depending on the dialect you were speaking, could have near-opposite meanings. One minister related a Sunday experience in which she had been invited to speak at a village across the island. She had been told that they would understand her Cebuano and that she didn't need a translator. Nothing could have been further from the truth: during the service people began talking to each other and some left because they couldn't understand her message!

The islands, analogous to the scattered beads of a "broken rosary," have uncommon hardships due to geography and language: transportation, communication, and governance are just some of the everyday challenges that many face. But the broken-rosary analogy goes beyond these obvious, daily impositions. There is centuries-old history behind the traffic officer's comment: Philippine cultural and political destiny and identity have not been indigenously shaped but formed by religious and national imperialisms of the worst kind. Karnow (1989) summarizes: "First came Spain and then the United States—or, as the neat summation of Philippine history goes: 'Three centuries in a Catholic convent and fifty years in Hollywood.'" A colony for 350 years, Spain and its Iberian Catholicism, and then the United States, left imprints that are deep, penetrating, and visible on every level of Philippine life.

Millennia before the West's arrival, fifteen thousand years ago, Mongoloid tribes from China arrived on the islands, followed by others from the Southeast Asian Rim. Around the time of Jesus' birth, Malays from Indonesia poured into the archipelago, eventually becoming the predominant ethnic population. (Karnow 1989, 38) Malay and Chinese physical features are visible in the faces and body types of most Filipinos: looking at a person's features can keep you guessing as to their dominant ethnic heritage—Chinese or Malay.

But this is where the guesswork ends. There are no questions about more recent Filipino heritage. On his way to find the precious spices of the West Indies, the Portuguese explorer Ferdinand Magellan stumbled onto the archipelago in 1521 after months of horrific adventures that claimed many of his crew's lives (at this point, he'd been at sea for over a year). So, desperate and thankful for an opportunity to rest, and feeling as though he'd been brought back from the dead, Magellan named the islands San Lazaro in honor of Lazarus whom Jesus had brought back to life. Magellan didn't rush ashore and was eventually greeted by a local chieftain named Humabon who steered the fleet to Cebu, where Magellan claimed the archipelago for God (Catholicism) and country (Spain). He followed the proclamation with an Easter sermon (complete with interpretation into Malay) praising Christianity and Catholic belief—at which point the natives agreed to convert! It is reported that Magellan wept for joy. In a week, two thousand natives, along with Humabon, were baptized, making the islands the only Christian nation in Asia. But Magellan's ecstasy would be short-lived: he would be murdered within a week. A neighboring chieftain, Lapu Lapu, grew suspicious of the attention being awarded to his traditional enemy, Humabon. With fifteen hundred armed warriors, Lapu Lapu lured Magellan and sixty of his crew into a trap from which only a handful escaped.

Renamed the Philippines by King Charles of Spain in honor of Crown Prince Philip II in 1542, the colony was eventually managed by New Spain (Mexico) for three hundred years, giving the islands the distinction of being a colony of a colony. A Spanish bureaucrat living in Mexico City, Miguel Lopez de Legazpi, was appointed by King Philip II to colonize the archipelago. Karnow (1989, 44) writes that Legazpi landed in 1565 (in Cebu, as had Magellan) with a "complement of three hundred and sixty men [which] included sailors, soldiers, lawyers, accountants and royal officials." The archipelago was carved up under the system of *encomienda:* large tracts of land, and the people living there, were awarded to Spanish loyalists known as the *principales.* Eventually, the *encomienda* system gave way to the hacienda system—plantations for the massive production of sugar, fruit, and tobacco. Under colonial rule, many Filipinos lost their land and were subjected to forced labor and exploitive taxes. Many of today's ruling and wealthy elite date their inheritances back to the system of *encomienda* when their families were members of the *principales.*

Among the administrative settlers on Legazpi's ships were "five Augustian priests [whose] mission [was] to 'bring to the natives . . . a knowledge of the Holy Catholic faith.'" The ruling bond between church and state was there from the beginning and by the seventeenth century five Catholic orders had carved up the islands with the Visayans going to the Jesuits (among the Visayans—the islands located in central Philippines—is Negros). Secular officials would come and go, but the church stayed.

Rome's surrogate was the local priest or friar, who exercised nearly unchecked power. He was overseer of the parish budget; he registered and taxed villagers as well as conducted the census; the barrio friar administered health care and public-works programs; he helped with military inscription, supervised the police and jail conditions. As village censor, he alone could ban anything he thought derogatory to church or state; he had the final word in all trials and village administrative decisions.

The barrio friar also oversaw all education, a supervision that had long-term, historical effects. Classes were conducted in the local dialect: experience had taught Spanish Catholics that when natives learned the imperial language they often felt empowered, leading to disruptive and rebellious behavior. Consequently, unlike other Spanish colonies, Filipinos never became a Spanish-speaking people. Not only that, but natives stayed largely uneducated. Shortly after the Spanish-American War (fought from February 15–May 1, 1898, and from which the United States acquired the Philippines, Guam, Cuba, and Puerto Rico), a survey showed that despite colonial boasts of barrio education, more than half the population was illiterate. (Karnow 1989, 53) Luis Francia (1993) summarizes the lack of educational preparation in this way: "The conquistador and the friar constituted a formidable duo, implanting the fear of God in brown breasts, teaching the *indios* praying charms to ward off the devil but lacking the same zeal in educating the masses. Higher education was reserved for the wellborn, the *ilustrados,* scions of transplanted Spanish families and of prominent Creole clans. Old World imperialists that they were, the Spanish disdained any notion of democracy, horrified by the thought of a brown-skinned people ever identifying with them. Whatever their faults they always made it perfectly clear how unattractive cross-cultural pollination was to them."

Illiteracy was rampant among the masses, but among the elite it was a different story—the wealthy sent their children to Spain to be educated. The newly well-educated Filipinos were dismayed to learn on their return that their status had not changed from the Spanish perspective. The main opponents to this end were the powerful religious movements that were personified in the friars. To stir up widespread mass support for their cause, the *ilustrados* focused on the friar-abuse that was so widespread. The Propaganda Movement was the result, but this push for democratic and nationalistic ideals met with harsh Spanish repression. An early leader of the Propa-

ganda Movement was the talented Philippine intellectual
Jose Rizal y Mercado, who was executed by colonial authorities in 1896 for inflammatory and relentless criticism of Spanish imperialism. Following his death, Emilio
Aguinaldo was chosen to lead the drive for independence.
In August 1897, he negotiated what he believed was an
equitable truce to end the rebellion—with some guaran-
tees for Filipinos—in return for his exile to Hong Kong. It
was from exile that Aguinaldo, as the recognized leader of
the anti-Spanish rebellion, struck a deal with the United
States—support the war against Spain for Philippine independence. Aguinaldo considered the United States an
ally and welcomed his new relationship with "The Great
American nation, the cradle of liberty, and therefore a
friend to our people." (Pimentel 1999) On May 7, 1898,
Aguinaldo returned to the Philippines following George
Dewey's defeat of the Spanish in Manila Bay. On June 12,
Aguinaldo declared independence from Spain, making
the Philippines Asia's first republic.

The guns on Admiral Dewey's ships in Manila Bay
had barely cooled before the Board of Foreign Missions of
the Presbyterian Church (USA) issued a report that included the following statement: " . . . the political and military relations into which the United States has been so
strangely forced with reference to the Philippine Islands
and also to Cuba and to Porto Rico, involve certain moral
and religious responsibilities—responsibilities which are
perhaps quite independent of the precise character of the
political relationships which may hereafter be formed
with them, and . . . the Christian people of America
should immediately and prayerfully consider the duty of
entering the door which God in His providence is thus
opening." (Sitoy 1989, 4) With Spanish Catholicism now a
fading authoritarian presence, American Protestantism
was ready to fill an anticipated void.

Discussion over what to do with the archipelago began immediately. But the intensity and urgency of the
debate ceased as Filipinos and Americans battled each

other for control of the colony's political and economic future. In February 1899, as the U.S. Senate was nearing a vote on Philippine annexation, "four Filipino soldiers crossing the San Juan Bridge near Manila were killed by U.S. forces, sparking the Philippine-American War, which is known in U.S. military annals as the 'Philippine Insurrection.' The clash sealed the vote for annexation in the Senate." (Wei and Kamel 1998) What some thought would be a simple, months-long skirmish turned into a long, brutal, and costly war. More than 100,000 American troops eventually would be involved in the fight for possession of the archipelago. U.S. leadership was not prepared for the outpouring of Philippine resistance to another imperial power. "So broad was the Filipino army's mass base that one American general declared: 'It may be necessary to kill half of the Filipinos in order that the remaining half of the population may be advanced to a higher plane of life than their present semi-barbarous state affords.'" (Pimentel 1999) Eventually, President Theodore Roosevelt declared the war over on July 4, 1902 (though fighting continued for several more years). The "insurrection" had claimed at least 250,000 lives—some estimate one million.

In June 1900, William Howard Taft arrived as the first civilian governor of the archipelago. On July 4, 1901, General Arthur MacArthur (father of Douglas) reluctantly gave up his post as military governor and Taft was officially installed. Months later, six hundred public school teachers from the States arrived aboard the U.S.S. *Thomas* to begin a massive colony-wide literacy program—in English. (They became known as Thomasites.) Francisco Sionil Jose, a Filipino novelist and publisher, notes: "The Spanish came carrying the Cross. The Americans marched behind the symbol of their secular religion—the schoolbook." (Kiester and Kiester 1999) With the United States tightening and widening its political and military control as well as spreading its social and cultural programs, Protestant missionaries could enter the archipelago with evangelical enthusiasm. Typical of the manifest-destiny fervor was Dr. George F. Penigore, who told the Presbyterian General Assembly: "We cannot ignore the fact that God has given into our hands, that is, into the hands of American Christians, the Philippine Islands, and thus opened a wide door and effectual to their populations, and has, by the very guns of our battleships, summoned us to go up and possess the land." (Sitoy 1989, 3)

But a queue was beginning to form: though they may have been the most publicly outspoken about it, the Presbyterians weren't the only ones eager to enter the archipelago. Some were quick to recognize that a rivalry was forming—a rivalry that could see a duplication of efforts and great expense. And so a new course was attempted, according to the Board of Foreign Missions of the Presbyterian Church in the U.S.A.: "We have heard much in recent years of the principle of comity, and we are earnestly striving to promote that comity in lands which are already jointly occupied. We believe that the new situation thus providentially forced upon us affords us excellent opportunity not only for beginning this work but for beginning it right from the viewpoint of Christian fellowship and the economical use of men and money." (Sitoy 1989, 5) Taking the initiative at comity were representatives from the Presbyterian, Congregational, Baptist, Methodist, Episcopal, and Reformed mission boards (of the United States and Canada). But as with Magellan's initial exuberance, the Protestant comity would be in for a rough start. In fact for decades Protestant missionaries, similar to the Catholic orders before them, tried to divide the archipelago into zones of missionary activity. The order and structure never lasted long, but resulted in turf battles, in part because all denominations were never present when the divisions were made. Each breakdown would require another meeting and another plan, often leading to a renewed ecumenical spirit that would eventually be lost due to more misunderstanding, jealously, or new but unwelcome missionaries.

The opening of the Philippines to Protestant missionary evangelism marked the beginning of what some have called the Philippine Protestant Reformation. Yet the parallel to Martin Luther's revolution breaks down because, unlike the fourteenth-century split from Catholicism, missionary Protestantism in the Philippines was simply one more example of colonial cultural imperialism, which is to say it did not come from within the archipelago, it was not a home-grown reformation, but a colonial imposition. Yet there was a Reformation of the Catholic Church whose leadership was Filipino. The Philippine Protestant Reformation was led by Bishop Gregorio Aglipay and Don Isabelo de los Reyes, Sr.

For years, Philippine rebellion movements had roots in religion. Decades of small resistance movements found their support and philosophies emerging from grass-roots interpretations of biblical themes and local rituals. Given this past, it is not surprising that in October 1899, filled with enthusiasm and idealism from their liberation from Spanish rule, Filipino clergy gathered and made provisional plans for an independent Philippine church. Gregorio Aglipay, a Roman Catholic priest with outstanding leadership ability as well as a lieutenant general in the Philippine national army, was made vicar general (at the time of his election he was fighting in the field against the Americans with a U.S. reward for his capture). In 1902, following the Philippine-American War, de los Reyes, president of the Philippine Labor Congress, urged that an independent church be formally established, thus making the 1899 provisional plans a reality. De los Reyes nominated Aglipay as bishop, and the church was named *Santa Iglesia Catholica Apostolica Filipina Independiente,* with Governor General Taft as vice president. American Unitarian Association President Louis Cornish (1942, 53–54) caught the spirit of the times when he wrote in *The Philippines Calling:* "Consider the beginnings. Two thousand laboring men dared dream of taking the friar-dominated Spanish Catholic Church in the Philippines, making it non-Roman and non-Spanish, reforming it, modernizing its teachings, and perpetuating it as the free and independent Church of the Islands. They dedicated themselves fearlessly to a free faith and free worship, and to science and research. I challenge you, find the equal of it!" This was the beginning of the Philippine Protestant Reformation.

The Reformation immediately had to overcome several obstacles. First, Americans viewed Aglipay and de los Reyes not as social and religious reformers, but as social and political radicals: Aglipay was an insurgent and de los Reyes a socialist, and together they were keeping alive the tradition set by early Philippine radical reformer Jose Rizal y Mercado. Rizal, who was martyred in 1896 for his public opposition to Spanish tyranny, and Aglipay had been fellow students—free-thinking, brilliant, and close friends. When it came time for Aglipay to consider the study of law, it was Rizal who urged him to pursue religion, and as he had done, to dream of promoting Filipino welfare by leading the people with inspiration and truth. Rizal promised Aglipay, "We will be oriental Quixotes, Quixotes of the mind!" (Cornish 1942, 106) Early in the Independent Church's life, Rizal was canonized a saint. When Aglipay and de los Reyes led the Philippine Protestant Reformation, the memory of Rizal's populist and revolutionary appeal as well as his friendship with Aglipay was still fresh in many minds. This memory, when added to the Independent Church's enthusiasm for a thoroughly national Filipino church, created an obstacle too threatening and confusing for U.S. Protestant missionary leadership—this wasn't the direction they believed was in the archipelago's best interests.

Another setback came when Aglipay and de los Reyes, shortly before their break from Rome, approached the Protestant missionaries of Manila seeking to explore cooperation or a union. After listening to their theology, their plans for and the condition of the Independent Church (in 1939, the government estimated that the Independent Church had 1.5 million members), the missionaries told them that any attempt to unite was impossible. Why? Though they didn't come right out and say it, it was because the Independent Church sounded too Roman Catholic. Yet it's hard to say who had a greater suspicion of and animosity for the Roman church,

American Protestants or the emerging Filipino church! After three hundred years of oppressive Spanish Catholic rule and teaching, it's unclear what Protestant missionaries expected. That American Protestantism was unwilling to work with the new church's leadership was not a promising sign.

The final obstacle the Independent Church confronted was over property rights. When they broke from Rome, they took many church buildings with them, believing that since it was the people of the communities who built the churches, they belonged to the community. And if that community chose to affiliate with the Independent Church and not the Roman Catholic Church, then the building went, too. Rome demanded restoration. In 1906, while the court deliberated, Governor Taft issued a proclamation of "Peaceful Possession," which kept church buildings in the hands of current occupants until litigation was completed. In 1908, the court ruled that the Philippine church property belonged to Rome. The decision was a major blow to the young church.

There are, of course, different versions regarding America's involvement with the Philippines. Immediately following the Spanish-American War, as well as after the Philippine-American War, there were calls for the archipelago's independence—many were uncomfortable with America's colonialist role. But none of the initiatives could ever overcome the strong and diverse opposition to freedom. Raymond Bonner (1987, 29) summarizes the organized opposition to Philippine independence: "The war was fought for businessmen who wanted new profits; generals who wanted bases; and other Americans who just wanted to do good—the 'white man's burden,' as Rudyard Kipling wrote in 1899. President William McKinley called it 'benevolent assimilation,' a policy designed to 'uplift and Christianize' Filipinos." Something always seemed to get in the way of freedom: Immediately following the war in 1898, there was the Philippine-American War; in 1902 when this war was declared over, isolated rebellions continued; finally in 1934, Congress passed the Philippine Independence Act, which called for a ten-year transition period to freedom, and in 1935 a Commonwealth Government was inaugurated—but of course World War II got in the way when Japan attacked the Philippines and Pearl Harbor simultaneously. Eventually, on July 4, 1946, the Philippines celebrated independence, although a U.S. military presence would linger at Clark Air Force Base and Subic Naval Base for decades due to the Cold War communist threat. In 1962, Philippine Independence Day was changed from July 4 to June 12 to commemorate Emilio Aguinaldo's—the nation's first president in 1899—declaration of independence from Spain as well as a way of distancing the nation from the United States. Writing of the U.S. colonial adventure in his essay "The Philippine Incident," Mark Twain captured the feelings of many for decades to come when he portrayed a Filipino, sitting in darkness, saying to himself: "There must be two Americas: one that sets the captive free, and one that takes a once-captive's new freedom away from him, and picks a quarrel with him with nothing to found it on; then kills him to get his land." (Francia 1993)

Spain and the United States have forever left their imprints on the Philippines. A century of American business, military, and political exploitation and subterfuge have helped to leave the Philippines economically, culturally, and socially challenged. But this is going beyond the story this book tells. While Spanish imperialism and Catholicism did loosen their grip in 1898, generations of Filipinos would be dependent on large, centralized institutions like the Church and the State—infrastructures Spain and Catholicism left behind wherever they had once ruled. In this context, the Philippine Protestant Reformation would be off to a rough start, yet the rosary had been broken. It was into this bead-broken archipelago that Unitarianism would make an early entrance and exit, only to be followed by the unlikely emergence of Universalism on a remote island near the equator.

Questions for Discussion

1. In this chapter we read: "Contrary to what many believe, Spanish is not the national language nor are you likely to hear it spoken anywhere." There are other assumptions and mistaken ideas that Americans have about the Philippines. What were some of the things you learned from this short introduction? Share your education about the Philippines.

2. Cornish and others distinguish between the reformation imposed by American Protestants and the indigenous reformation/rebellion led by Aglipay. The thrust of American missionary zeal described in this chapter has often given overseas evangelism a negative image. In terms of the turn of the century context portrayed here, describe your reaction to Cornish's comment: "[The Philippine religious reformers] dedicated themselves fearlessly to a free faith and free worship, and to science and research. I challenge you, find the equal of it!"

3. "Spain and the United States have forever left their imprints on the Philippines." From your reading and experience, how has the Philippine colonial experience been different from others?

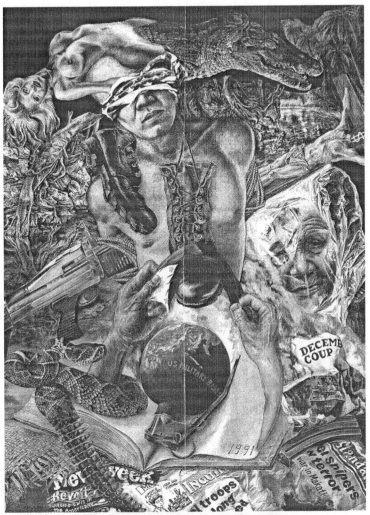

AMERIKANSER
It Kills!

1991 anti-USA poster: "Americanization—It Kills!"

Chapter 2

Unitarianism in the Philippines

If our Church has been able to offer the Filipinos such a rapid transition from Roman Catholicism to Rationalistic Christianity, it has been due in great measure to the liberal writings of our National Heroes. We trust that our Independent Church will continue its work of enlightenment and progress forever.

—Isabelo de los Reyes, Sr., Bishop of Manila, 1939

From the beginning of the Philippine Protestant Reformation there was a Unitarian presence. In 1900, William Howard Taft, an Ohio judge and active Unitarian (he would eventually be the president of the General Conference of Unitarian and Other Christian Churches as well as a significant member of the Unitarian Layman's League), was appointed by U.S. President McKinley to Manila as the archipelago's first civilian governor. In 1902 Taft was asked to be vice president of the Philippine Independent Church (PIC), and he accepted. When Taft returned to the Philippines as secretary of state in 1907, he brought with him Unitarian literature for Aglipay and de los Reyes. (Sienes 1994a) Though we might assume that Taft and the PIC's leadership conversed about religion—about Unitarianism—the only thing we know for sure is that following the Spanish-American war, Aglipay and de los Reyes quickly distanced themselves from the rigidity of Spanish Catholicism. As the separation from Spain and Rome widened, their free-thinking theology and liberal religious leanings emerged stronger and clearer.

The origin of Aglipay's liberal Christianity grew out of his long-time friendship with Philippine national hero and PIC saint Jose Rizal y Mercado. In *The Religious Thought of Dr. Jose Rizal,* Eugene A. Hessell (as documented by Rebecca Quimada Sienes [1994a]) reports that Rizal, though he never wrote any theological works, had a great interest in religion. Hessell drew the following composite of Rizal's theology:

- He believed in a God interdependent with the cosmos.
- He believed God gave humans the gift of reason and conscience.
- He believed humans have inherent worth and dignity.
- He believed Jesus taught God's love by word and example.
- He believed that followers of Jesus' religion should treat every human with dignity and respect.
- He believed that individuals should serve the whole community.
- He believed that deeds, not creeds, are the heart of religious living, and that worship should be simple.

Of course, Rizal's theology was framed by an oppressive and punitive Spanish Catholic culture—it influenced even the most liberal thinkers. Yet in Rizal's theology are found the seeds of liberal religion—quite free-thinking for the time! It's here where we discover the origins of Aglipay's liberal unitarian Christianity—views that would ostracize and isolate him and de los Reyes and the Independent Church from mainline Protestantism.

Well-documented are the PIC's conversations with mainline Protestant groups. After failing to gain a union with Manila Protestant missionaries in 1901, Aglipay and de los Reyes approached the Protestant Episcopal Church (USA) and the Swiss National Church in 1904. But like the earlier Manila meeting, there were unresolved theological issues for both groups. In fact, disagreement, rejection, and/or suspicion would be a pattern for nearly forty years. The Independent Church was unaffiliated with if not shunned by mainline Christian denominations: the PIC didn't want association with

Roman Catholicism, and mainline Protestantism found them "too Roman in ritual, too rationalistic in theology, too Spanish in ethics, and too independista in politics." (Cornish 1942, 55) In his short history of Protestantism in the Philippines, T. Valentino Sitoy, Jr. (1989, 127), writes about one of the Church's significant theological liabilities: "The entry of Unitarian ideas into its official documents pulled the Philippine Independent Church away from the mainstream catholic tradition, until Bishop Isabelo de los Reyes, Jr., who strongly espoused trinitarianism, became Supreme Bishop in 1947." Similar to the way Unitarian Christianity co-opted Boston's King's Chapel and later many of the New England trinitarian churches, Aglipay and de los Reyes espoused a unitarian theology that transformed PIC doctrine yet left the church's Roman liturgy and ritual unchanged. While there was no official institutional Unitarian affiliation, the Philippine trinitarian Protestants perceived the Church's liberal religious leanings as unacceptable. Some Unitarian recognition would eventually come.

A Congregational minister serving in the Philippines, Dr. Frank Laubach was home for a visit in the States when he met Dr. John Lathrop, a Unitarian minister. Laubach told Lathrop about the work being done by Aglipay and de los Reyes resulting in the creation of a Philippine Protestant Reformation. Lathrop shared the story with Louis Cornish, president of the American Unitarian Association (AUA), who saw this as an opportunity to spread the liberal gospel in Asia. In 1928, Lathrop and Dr. Curtis Reese visited Aglipay on a trip to India. Others, including Rev. Eugene Shippen, Rev. Berkeley Blake, and Rev. Jazeb Sutherland, visited the Philippines in the 1920s and 1930s. In 1931 and 1934, Aglipay and de los Reyes came to the United States. Their trips included visits to Unitarian churches with AUA President Cornish. During his first visit, Aglipay was awarded an honorary doctorate in divinity by Meadville Theological School. The second visit coincided with their attendance at the Trien-

nial Congress of the International Association for Liberal
Christianity and Religious Freedom (IALCRF—predecessor to the International Association of Religious Free-
dom), of which the PIC was a member. Shippen and Blake reported to Cornish that though
the development of the new church was slowly evolving,
the leadership was committed and wise: "Give them time,
give them encouragement," they advised Cornish. In 1937,
Cornish was elected president of the IALCRF and it was
soon after this election that he made an extended trip to
the Philippines as a guest of the Independent Church. A
description of this trip is recounted in his book *The Philippines Calling,* published in 1942.* In his book, Cornish
quotes from de los Reyes's brief statement "The Position
of the Independent Church," written for Cornish's book at
the request of Aglipay:

> Our Church has retained from the Roman Catholic
> Church all that was found reasonable and harmless. The
> vestments and many of its magnificent ceremonies, that
> possess so great an appeal for the Filipinos and other artis-
> tic peoples, were retained, but with a rational interpreta-
> tion. What is a myth to science must be a myth to us.
> Rejecting all ecclesiasticism, we preserve the real teachings

---

* Though Cornish and his wife made their visit in 1939, *The Philippines Calling* was not published until after the United States entered
the war, probably because the book is filled with inflammatory anti-
Japan rhetoric. For example, in the introduction Cornish writes: "The
best time to quench a fire is when it starts. The best way to prevent the
arrival of the Japanese at Seattle and San Francisco and Los Angeles
and ultimately along the whole Pacific Coast, is to drive them from the
Philippines. Once the millions of Japanese have settled on the islands,
it matters little what the men around the peace table may some day
decree. They never could be dislodged. Japan would want the best
terms she could get while she laughs at her enemies. In a generation
or two the Philippines would racially be hers." (x–xi) Still early in the
war, perhaps the book's publisher, Dorrance and Company, believed
that attack by Japan was not as inevitable as Cornish (and others)
thought: Why publish a book with such provocative language unless
the risk is over?

of Jesus: "Love to God and of our fellow beings." We retain images on our altars, just as the American Unitarians have retained the figures of saints in stained glass windows, but not for worship. The images to us are only reminders of the eminent virtues of the persons represented.

We maintain always that modern science must inspire our doctrines; hence since our establishment we have declared that through evolution man has become what he is to-day. We admit no miracles. We believe in God as the Mysterious Energy that keeps the Universe and that gives life and directs all beings. We always have maintained that the Bible has many interpolations and inaccuracies. Yet we consider the Bible as a holy book with many excellent lessons. We believe that all the scriptures of the world contain good. (79–80)

De los Reyes's statement reads like an introduction pamphlet for Unitarian Christianity, perhaps just as liberal as many AUA congregations of that era. Cornish was enthusiastic about what he read, heard, and saw. He did as much as he could to generate interest in the AUA to seek support for the Independent Church. He had announced their need, their like-minded theology, and historical, worldwide impact in *The Philippines Calling,* but no one was answering his call. The AUA's Commission of Appraisal report, *Unitarians Face a New Age* (1936), had anticipated this lack of response—what must have been a discouraging setback to Cornish's hard work and hopes. The report concluded: "The plain fact is that most Unitarians are lamentably indifferent to this whole subject. The international aspect of our denominational program is most inadequately financed. Even the moral support which it receives is scattered and half-hearted. It is as though the ordinary Unitarian church were so completely absorbed in the conduct of its own affairs that it had no time and energy to devote to larger considerations. This is a most unfortunate condition, which requires vigorous effort to correct it." (19) (See Appendix 1 for AUA's Commission of Appraisal report on the Philippines.)

Even though the Philippine Independent Church was nearly four decades old when Bishop Aglipay died in 1940, it was still structurally immature and unable to withstand the loss of his charismatic leadership. By 1946 there were serious governance issues that divided the Church into factions. Each faction had its own supreme bishop, council, and assembly and claimed to be the one and true independent church. In 1947, under the leadership and guidance of de los Reyes, Jr., the Independent Church broke from its theological heritage by adopting a trintarian Declaration of Faith and entered negotiation with the Protestant Episcopal Church for the apostolic succession of its clergy. In April 1948, three PIC bishops were consecrated at the Cathedral of St. Luke in Manila. The issue of division eventually made its way to the Philippine Supreme Court, which in 1955 ruled that the faction led by Bishop Isabelo de los Reyes, Jr., was the valid *Iglesia Filipina Independiente.* In 1961, the Philippine Episcopal Church and the Independent Church signed a concordat of intercommunion.

Though there were several smaller factions that split from the PIC, the spirit and theology of Aglipayan Unitarian Christianity appears to have come to rest with the Independent Church of Filipino Christians (ICFC), the group that was on the losing end of the Supreme Court's 1955 judgment. When PIC and ICFC disagreements and hostilities erupted in violence and criminal action, a group broke from the ICFC that organized as the Philippine Unitarian Church (PUC). Like the ICFC, the PUC followed the doctrines set down by Bishop Aglipay. They adopted the motto: "Be a Unitarian to be a true Aglipayan." The ICFC participates in the International Association of Religious Freedom.

There's no sure way to know what might have happened had the AUA, as Cornish desired, committed resources to aiding and strengthening Aglipay and de los Reyes and their vision of the Independent Church. What we know for sure is that the AUA made no commitment of any kind: we also know that the vision of Philippine Unitarian Christianity as described by Cornish and de los Reyes in *The Philippines Calling* died in 1947 when de los Reyes, Jr., led the PIC into the trinitarian fold.

This would not be the end of liberal religion in the Philippines. Not on Luzon, but on the island of Negros, in the central Visayans, 300 miles south of Manila, liberal religion was emerging in the mountains in the personality of a Pentecostal preacher.

Questions for Discussion

1. What is your reaction to Rizal's theology and how it might have shaped the Philippine Independent Church?

2. "Give them time, give them encouragement" was the advice offered by early Unitarian visitors to the Philippine Independent Church. The PIC received neither. What do you think happened? What do you think was the source of the indifference cited in the Commission of Appraisal report?

3. It was estimated that the Philippine Independent Church had 4 million members. Imagine: Had the AUA voted to establish faith ties with the PIC, how might this have shaped Unitarian Universalist history and future?

Gregorio Aglipay

Chapter 3

Universalism in the Philippines

"Maglipay Universalist"

Chorus:
To teach the hope that is for all,
Proclaim the Universal call.
To teach the hope that is for all,
Proclaim the Universal call.

Be joyful, Universalists, Come celebrate this company.
Officials, members all unite, Rejoicing in debate that's
 free.
To teach the Universal light, To strengthen our
 democracy.

Heaven is Universalist, For everyone from rich
 to poor.
We are not chosen from a list, To enter through the
 heavenly door.
Lift up your hearts to God's great grace, That beckons
 every race to soar.

The rigid Bible worshippers, Restrict our God to
 ancient days.
The priests, the Pope, the Calvinists, Are preaching
 far too narrow ways.
Remember Universalists, The sun of God has
 many rays.

—Toribio Quimada, 1917–1988
Lyricized by Richard Boeke, 1989
Edited by Eugene Navias

While the diversity reflected in physical features, language, education, and geography make it virtually impossible to speak of Filipinos with broad characterizations and labels, there is a context and condition most Filipinos have experienced. No one can avoid the deep-seated everyday influence of Spanish Catholicism's legacy. Though its grip on daily life has weakened, its diminished influence still permeates nearly all aspects of Filipino living. The legacy is most noticeable and felt in the *barangays,* the small villages where many islanders live. In her unpublished paper on the history of liberal religion on Negros island, Rebecca Quimada Sienes (1994b) quotes Teodoro A. Agoncillo who, in *The History of the Filipino People,* describes the life experienced by *barangay* residents: "The friars control all the fundamental forces of society. They control the educational system, for they own schools, and are the local inspectors of every primary school. They control the minds of the people because in a dominantly Catholic country, the parish rectors can utilize the pulpit and confessionals to publicly or secretly influence the people; they control all the municipal and local authorities and the medium of communication; and they execute all the orders of the central government. . . . "

These are the conditions, history, and legacy on the island of Negros, the home of Philippine Universalism. Located between Luzon and Mindanao in the cluster of islands called the Visayans, bordered by Cebu and Panay, Negros is approximately 125 miles long and on the average about 40 miles wide (Negros is about 390 miles south of Manila). The island's interior is hilly to mountainous, and dramatically slopes to the sea within short distances of the coastline. From many mountaintops, there are panoramic views that include lush green hills and jungle-dotted fields of sugarcane and rice paddies, and forests of bamboo, banana, and mango groves, while in the distance is the ocean, with small one- or two-person fishing boats.

While sugarcane has been king on Negros for centuries, rice is also grown, though economics and its growing season make sugarcane more profitable. Cane, rice, and fishing make up the economy of Negros. In the *barangays,* it's common to see men walking out of the village in the dim of early morning, machete in belt, on their way to a pick-up location or heading directly to the fields to harvest sugarcane in much the same way it has been done for centuries—by hand. Many of these folk may also own or lease 1 or 2 hectares (1 hectare is equivalent to 2.5 U.S. acres) where they grow rice for their family and/or friends. A daily diet includes rice at least three times a day along with dried fish and local fruit. Chicken, goat, or pig is a treat often reserved for special occasions.

The *barangay* is the center of life on Negros, as it is in the Philippines. During Spanish rule, the small villages were called barrios, but the name was changed back to the traditional *barangay* by President Ferdinand Marcos. A *barangay* was the long Malay boat used by the very early settlers of the archipelago. As they would reach land, settlements were established by boatload—family and friends in one *barangay* or several boats would stay together as a unit, becoming a village. Though there might be distance between them, these *barangays* would eventually compose the small villages of a township. As part of the Marcos government's desire to further distance the nation from its colonial past, *barangay* became the official nomenclature.* Each village has an elected *barangay* cap-

---

* While the renaming of villages as *barangays* has become accepted vocabulary and a source of pride, Marcos's desire and ability to wrap himself in Philippine nationalism often went to unprecedented and creative—if not suspect—lengths. Of interest here is his connection to Aglipay. Karnow writes: "As [Marcos] told it, [he] renounced Catholicism to follow Gregorio Aglipay, a nationalist priest who defied the Vatican to found a revolutionary church. Marcos escaped unscathed from World War II, he said, because Aglipay had given him an *anting anting,* an amulet made of magic wood that rendered its holder invisible." (1989, 367) Consider the possibilities: Had the Aglipayan church survived as Unitarian and had Marcos remained active in the Independent Church (if this was true), he would be added to the list of notable Unitarian world leaders—King John Sigismund, Thomas Jefferson, Ferdinand Marcos!

tain, treasurer, and council, a *barangay* hall, and a day care center where families can leave their children as they go to work. Many *barangays* have an elementary school, though it's common, especially in very remote areas, for several *barangays* to share a school. Most public high schools are regional, though private high schools are usually close to the sponsoring institution (e.g., a church or university). Private high schools charge tuition which, for most, place them out of possibility.

Negros is composed of two provinces that unequally split the island between west and east: Negros Occidental (population 2.5 million) and Negros Oriental (population 1 million). The provincial capital of Occidental is Bacolod, located on the northwest coast; Dumaguete City is the provincial capital of Negros Oriental and is located on the southeast coast. Bacolod is the larger of the two. It looks and feels like a city ("It even has taxis!" one friend told me with great excitement): several city centers, a sports arena, paved streets, office buildings and factories, suburbs—all with an urban pace. Maps of the Philippines always include Bacolod.

Dumaguete (headquarters for the Unitarian Universalist Church of the Philippines), while a city and a provincial capital, has the appearance of a large town. It feels as though it's trying to decide if it really likes what must eventually come with being an urban political, academic, and economic center; there is a resistance that is being worn down by the inevitability of size, activity, and years. An indication of the challenging tensions resulting from growth is seen in the mainstay of Dumaguete transportation, the motorcab, a motorcycle with a covered two-wheeled passenger car attached (often called a pedicab, but a pedicab is actually a bicycle with an attached passenger cab). Each car can comfortably carry two to four people, depending on both the size of the cab and the number of people. Additional passengers ride on laps, on "running boards," on the motorcycle, or anywhere else the driver deems okay (which is virtually anyplace the passenger can hang on. I never heard a motorcab driver say,

"No, you can't ride because there isn't enough room"—it was always up to the prospective passenger to figure out where to fit in). Room can also be made for luggage, groceries, livestock, or housewares. I have seen as many as ten in/on a motorcab, especially students, who seem to take great delight in getting as many on a cab as possible; I rode in motorcabs carrying human and farmyard passengers, crops, and garden supplies; I traveled in motorcabs carrying families and friends and all their day's needs as they headed for the beach or mountain parks. Motorcabs are an easy and inexpensive way to get around, albeit it noisy, smelly, often subject to breakdown (they are driven until they are well beyond repair), and unprotected in poor conditions (extreme heat, rain, or dust which, depending on the season, can be the norm).

A couple of decades ago, the principal mode of transportation in Dumaguete was a horse-drawn cart or carriage. Then came pedicabs (which are still prevalent in *barangays,* smaller towns, or certain sections of the city). With each of these there was no diesel odor, they were quieter, and since the city was smaller there wasn't the need for as many. Now there are motorcycle-powered motorcabs, and there are hundreds (maybe thousands) of them, all licensed by the city and usually owned by large motorcab companies (though many are privately owned). On a weekday, Dumaguete streets are congested with public buses as well as delivery and sugarcane trucks— the national highway goes through the center of Dumaguete. All of them impatiently wait on the volume of snail-paced motorcabs, while the growing number of private cars honk their horns at the motorcyclists who, often carrying one or two and sometimes three passengers, weave in and out and around the slower, waiting, or stalled traffic. Several years ago one traffic light was installed at a busy intersection just outside of the city center as an experiment, a sign of better things to come. It was a disaster and the light was removed shortly after its installation—it created too much confusion! So there are no traffic lights, but there are traffic officers who try to

keep everyone moving at a reasonable flow. A recent city
plan recommended abolishing the motorcab industry to
be replaced by automobile taxis, as in Bacolod. The plan
was rejected when motorcab drivers packed the meeting
in protest, claiming that motorcab transportation was
economical for the poor and students, was one of the
largest employers, and was a trademark of Dumaguete
life: to do away with motorcabs would be like robbing the
provincial capital of a claim to fame (like San Francisco's
trolleys, Chicago's "El," or Boston's "T"). So the motorcabs
stay, though many drivers admit that their days are numbered: Dumaguete is growing, automobile taxis can be
seen, and motorcabs don't appear to be in the future.

In the heart of Dumaguete City, in a park-like environment of green lawns and broad, 100-year old acacia
shade trees, is the academic jewel of Negros: Silliman
University, a small, private, liberal arts college founded
in 1901 by the Board of Foreign Missions of the Presbyterian Church (USA)—the Presbyterians had been
granted missionary "rights" to Negros Oriental. Begun as
the Silliman Institute for elementary education with
gifts from New York philanthropist Dr. Horace Brinsmade
Silliman, in 1910 the government awarded it the right to
grant degrees. By 1921 it had established its Bible School
in cooperation with the American Board of Commissioners for Foreign Missions, representing the Congregational
Church of the United States. The Institute became a University in 1935 and the Bible School's affiliation para-
lleled the union of mainline Protestant churches, which
by 1948 was comprised of the United Church of Christ in
the Philippines (the union was led by the Presbyterian
and Congregational churches). After several renamings,
in 1966 the Institute was finally renamed The Divinity
School of Silliman University (called by many SUDS: Silliman University Divinity School). The Divinity School offers two degree programs. The six-year Bachelor of
Divinity program is for high school graduates and consists of two years of pretheology in liberal arts studies,
three years of intensive theological studies, and one year

of supervised internship. The other is the standard four-year Master of Divinity program, made up of three years of graduate theological studies and one year of supervised internship. The university never adopted any "articles of faith." Consequently, despite its rich Protestant heritage, it remains independent and nondenominational—hence its uniqueness and gift to the Philippines, and to the Unitarian Universalist Church of the Philippines (UUCP), which has had an ongoing relationship with the Divinity School for many years.

While all of the UUCP's congregations are on Negros, its history and leadership began on the island of Cebu, the birthplace of Toribio Sabandija Quimada. Born into a Roman Catholic family in 1917, Quimada was the second of seven brothers and six sisters. Zoilo, his father, was a farmer and carpenter of Spanish heritage. His mother, Juliana, was a mixture of Spanish and Malay heritages. As is still a common way, especially among rural Filipinos, the Quimada family of thirteen children was as much an economic necessity as a religious obligation—all helped in the daily household chores and farming. There was not much value given to education beyond the basics learned at the elementary level—besides, nearly every *barangay* had an elementary school, whereas high school and college meant not only travel but often cost (as described earlier, this is still the situation today).

Following marriage and during the Depression, Quimada moved to Nataban, San Carlos City, in Negros Oriental. Soon after their move, Quimada had his first exposure to a faith other than Roman Catholicism: he and his wife, Sergia, were living with a cousin who was an elder in the Presbyterian Church. It was here that he read the Bible for the first time, something that had not been permitted in Catholicism (though for many it was not read simply due to illiteracy). A turning point in his faith development came in 1937. Recalling this moment, Rebecca Quimada Sienes, his daughter, quotes her father: "After a long period of waiting and longing, the time had come for me to read this precious book, The Holy Bible.

This is the most valuable possession I ever had and will ever have in my life. Through this, I will learn the story of the Prophets, Patriarchs, Apostles, and Jesus Christ." (1994b, 5) Shortly following, Quimada left the Roman Catholic Church and began worshipping at a nearby congregation of *Iglesia Universal de Cristo*—which was not on the approved list of churches given to Quimada by his father! "It took several years for my family to recognize and accept the new faith that I embraced. During these times, my father would usually initiate a religious debate with me about my new faith. He would ignite this debate even in the presence of the people in our community, in our household, and in the presence of my friends." (1994b, 5–6) Still not a member, but because of his enthusiasm and grasp of the faith, Quimada was asked to teach Sunday school and occasionally preach. In 1943, the Quimada family (even his parents) became members of *Iglesia Universal de Cristo*. Five years later, as his ability and faith deepened and the local minister's health deteriorated, Quimada was called to the ordained ministry by the church's leader. He was ordained and commissioned with responsibility for nine *barangay* congregations.

One of the most frustrating aspects of his ministry was the lack of resources. While members might have their own bibles, there were religious education materials and hymnbooks that were also needed, and the church did not provide any. Consequently, Quimada had to make use of whatever he could find. In 1951, a new resource arrived by mail in a most out-of-the-ordinary way. He received a letter wrapped in an old newspaper from a leader in a congregation he served requesting a baptism for a church family. What a surprise to find that the newspaper wrapper included a listing of Protestant denominations in the United States: "He immediately went to the letter 'I' for "iglesia" then to the letter 'U' hoping to find *Iglesia Universal de Cristo*. Instead, what he found was the Univeralist Church of Wisconsin." (Sienes 1994b, 7)

He wrote to the listed address but his letter went unanswered. Months later, after being given an almanac, he found another reference to Universalism, this time for a Univeralist Church in Gloucester, Massachusetts. Another letter was sent and this one was answered by Rev. Carl Westman, who told Quimada that he had sent his inquiry on to Rev. Carleton Fisher, Executive Director of the Universalist Service Committee. That was in 1952. In the years that followed, Rev. Dana E. Klotzle, who succeeded Fisher, worked closely with Quimada to support his growing movement. (Klotzle 1956, 190)

Not only curiosity but his growing desire for educational as well as any supplemental religious material was a prime factor in Quimada's searching out the Universalist Church in America. Though it was never his intention to leave *Iglesia Universal de Cristo,* his budding relationship with Universalism was just the beginning of Quimada's odyssey: "[His] desire for religious education materials such as books, hymnbooks, children's books, and other items was realized through the Universalist Church in America. He wrote, 'This made me and my church members happy because there are materials for the children as well as for the adults.' His first adult textbook was *How to Know Your Bible.*" (Sienes 1994b, 8)

Quimada preached that a loving God is not capable of preparing a place called hell for the people to be tormented forever with fire. How could a loving God damn humanity? "He preached that the contradictions found in the Bible are proof that the Holy Bible is not the Word of God but an inspired book written by inspired people. He preached that Jesus Christ is not the Son of God, rather a gifted son of Joseph and Mary, who is divinely commissioned to be the messenger of God's message of justice, equality, and compassion. He preached that it is beyond the human conception to prove that Mary conceived Jesus through the Holy Spirit. Scientifically, it is illogical and unfounded and against human nature." (Ibid., 8–9)

Rev. Quimada's newfound and well-spoken religious liberalism was not popular with the leadership of *Iglesia Universal de Cristo.* Quimada's supervisor wrote a letter to Manila asking that Quimada's license as a minister in

IUC be annulled because he was not preaching and teaching the church's faith, but had come to rely on other teachings and sources—Universalism. His license was revoked and, as national law dictates, he was barred from practicing his ministry. In 1954, he was excommunicated by his church, leaving him and the nine congregations he served hurt, angry, and frustrated.

On May 18, 1954, Quimada requested the aid of a Universalist missionary to help him organize on Negros. The Universalist Church in America (UCA) responded that though they did not have missionaries, they would lend any assistance they could. That winter, preparations for recognition began and by spring all the paperwork was in order. On April 25, 1955, the Universalist Church of the Philippines (UCP) was registered with the Securities and Exchange Commission of the Republic of the Philippines. In that same year, Rev. Toshio Yoshioka, a Universalist minister from Japan, visited Negros and made his report to the UCA in Boston: "More than 90% of the people of the Philippines are Catholic. There are some Protestants, but they are strictly orthodox, strongly conditioned with the fear that because of Adam's fall they will go to hell after death. Thus, Mr. Quimada and his people were surprised and relieved by the Universalist teaching of universal salvation and the idea of a loving God rather than an angry god. In fact I was asked time and time again if they could really be saved, and as to what Universalism taught about Jesus (God or Man) and about the Bible. It seems to me that they are recapitulating the same experiences of the very early Universalists. They may be far behind the modern movement in Universalism, but they are on the right track of the history of the Universalist Church." (Ibid., 13) The first Universalist Church of the Philippines convention was held in Nataban, April 23–27, 1955. The annual convention continues to be held that week, always concluding with a celebration of Quimada's birthday on April 27.

Quimada's ministry did not stop with the nine congregations that followed him to Universalism. With financial

assistance from the Universalist Service Committee, he
began evangelizing. Rebecca Quimada Sienes recalls:
"Equipped with the public address system, hymnbooks
and Bibles, Rev. Quimada's preaching group left very early
on Saturday in order to be in Quezon before lunch time for
public preaching. Quezon is about a four hour walk. The
preaching group consisted of my father, one or two Elders
of the church, young women and men. While the young
people provided songs with guitar accompaniment, my father preached. If there was an Elder of the church present,
he preached too. Rev. Quimada preached extemporane-
ously for more or less one hour. His best topics for public
preaching included: Universal salvation for all humankind; Hell is hatred to your neighbors, heaven is love
to them; Jesus the Son of God or Man? His audience was a
[diverse group]. It was not unusual that someone from the
audience would ignite a religious discussion with Rev.
Quimada at the end of the program. I was always a witness to that, and he loved it." (1994b, 14–15)

In 1958, Quimada's life took another turn: On the recommendation of Rev. Yoshioka, the Universalist Service
Committee provided funds for Quimada to enroll at Silliman University in Dumaguete. It wasn't easy for him
since his education had stopped at seventh grade. In addition, he was trying to care for his family, and his congregations now numbered twenty-one. The load eventually
was too much and he settled for returning to high school
and finishing the final two years. Yet he did return to complete college. In 1960 he enrolled at Fountainhead University in Dumaguete, where he received his B.S. degree
in 1965. It was during these college years that he translated *Hymns of the Spirit* into Cebuano, the dialect of Negros Oriental.

With his work done in Dumaguete, he purchased some
land in the *barangay* of Nagbinlod, Santa Catalina, which
is south of Dumaguete in the mountains. The area is fer-
tile for sugarcane growing. He moved the UCP headquarters to the *barangay* where his ministry would take yet a

new direction: social activism and land reform. Many of
the poor farmers had inherited their land as family plots
handed down over generations. It was often undeeded,
which provided a loophole for corporations or wealthy
families to move in and take over. Quimada was angered
by local authorities who stood by and watched as poor
farming families lost their land and with it everything
they had. He began assisting these families by filing peti-
tions and completing the necessary paperwork required
to deed their land to them. Eventually, he ran for Nagbinlod Barangay Captain but lost as a result of massive
vote buying and the opposition's slogan, "If you vote for
Quimada you will become a Universalist," * a threat that
had a fearsome, penetrating power within the Catholic
authoritarianism and government oppression of Negros
in the 1960s. While his efforts on behalf of poor farmers—
like himself—would not stop, Quimada did not run for
public office again. He put his energy into strengthening
the Univeralist Church of the Philippines, which would
often mean siding with the peasant poor. It was this justice ministry and its high visibility that would eventually
lead to his death.

In 1972, the Church became a member of the International Association for Religious Freedom (IARF). (Aglipay's Independent Church had belonged to the IARF's
predecessor, the International Association for Liberal
Christianity and Religious Freedom, as did subsequent
groups who claimed to be in the Aglipayan tradition. The
UCP is also thought to be in that tradition though it developed independent of it.) The relationship with IARF
would develop into a crucial one for the Church, with
the UCP actively leading and participating in local, regional, and international IARF events as well as receiving

---

* In 1999, the Nagbinlod Barangay Captain is the village's Unitarian
Universalist minister and is addressed as "Rev. Captain Rafael Vibar."
He and Rev. Quimada were close friends.

generous and encouraging support in a variety of income-generating efforts such as husbandry and fishing. Instrumental to the Church's future was the IARF support it received for high school scholarships, one of the many ways the UCP had of supporting youth from *barangay* congregations. Some of these youth went on to become Divinity School students. As part of his ongoing efforts to improve the economic lives of the Church's members, Quimada, with IARF backing and local nonprofit help, established a church cooperative credit union that provided low-interest loans for additional projects as well as crisis needs (due to health or death). In 1984, the IARF awarded Quimada with the Albert Schweitzer Award for Distinguished Service. In 1988, IARF participation in the Philippines was unified by the organization of a Philippine chapter. The organizational meeting, held in Manila, was attended by representatives of the IARF, the UCP, the Bataan Catholic Youth Civic Circle, and the Independent Church of Filipino Christians (one of the Aglipayan splinter groups). The next year, due to the organizational leadership of Rebecca Quimada Sienes, the Philippines chapter held its conference at Silliman University.

For the Unitarian Universalist Church of the Philippines ("Unitarian" was added in 1985, as will be discussed in the next chapter), 1988 was an important year: IARF participation, the continuing growth of the movement, and the anticipated attendance by Rev. Quimada at the Unitarian Universalist Association General Assembly in Palm Springs, California, all were events that made the future of the UUCP very bright. But all of these milestones would be overshadowed by the untimely death of Quimada. In the early hours of May 23, the Quimada home was set on fire. While Quimada's family fled the home, Quimada stayed behind—for what reasons we will never know, though there is speculation that there were assassins there: gunfire was heard from the blazing house and after the fire was extinguished by a rain, Quimada's body was found. There would eventually be many explanations for what happened, but for most it was not difficult to understand: Quimada had been murdered for his justice-making ministry on behalf of poor farmers. Decades of oppression had set the scene for this tragic, life-taking event. From the 1970s through the early 1990s, the government perceived a threat to the status quo from the New People's Army, largely composed of rural poor (and branded as a "Communist threat"). Military troops were stationed throughout the Negros countryside (and on other islands), with checkpoints and patrols everywhere. A common military practice was village "cleansing": if a *barangay* was thought to be harboring antigovernment supporters (poor farmers thought to be sympathetic to the New People's Army), all residents were told that they had to move to other land (usually inferior land). Anyone left in the *barangay* would be arrested or shot as the enemy. Many villagers lost their land or never returned during these massive relocation efforts, a process that Quimada found outrageous—and he shared his outrage with many. It was this sort of activism that led the government troops to suspect him of being a left-wing supporter, which he wasn't. He supported poor farmers and their families who had for so long been abused by wealthy landowners and oppressed by local officials.

His death was attributed to the fire, officially recorded as an accident. But after the initial shock, the Quimada family began the arduous, complicated, and risky process of having Rev. Quimada's body exhumed and examined a second time to determine the real cause of death. The family and witnesses testified that there were sufficient reasons to believe that the fire was not the cause. When I visited in 1991, the exhumation proceedings were still going on and would continue for years.* Even though one of the six murderers had confessed and two were already

---

* During my 1991 visit, and during a previous visit by Unitarian Universalist colleague Fritz Hudson, this case received a lot of attention. Within hours of landing in Dumaguete City, I was taken to the family's attorney to discuss the case. Every other day we did something related to the exhumation/autopsy litigation.

in jail for other crimes, and while the whereabouts of others was known, obstacles to the exhumation and autopsy grew and grew. Finally Quimada's body was exhumed, the autopsy performed, and the death certificate corrected to say death by gunshots. Eleven years later, the murder investigation (or lack of an investigation) continues. Rev. Quimada's daughter, Rebecca, suggests that the same conditions that led to her father's death prevent the case from proceeding to a conclusion: "I worked hard to seek justice for the horrible death of my father. It is sad to say that when a poor person is fighting for justice, justice is usually denied. Justice is denied because the poor people cannot afford to hire a private lawyer; justice is denied because there are tons of cases for a dozen public defenders. It might not be fair to say, but a fair legal system is only for those who have power, money and status." (1994b, 25) There is the option of a "human rights" lawyer, but generally such a lawyer is considered left-wing and radical, and a sure way of drawing attention to you and your case—the kind of attention that would put the Quimada family, their friends, the UUCP, and of course the attorney at great risk.

The Unitarian Universalist Church of the Philippines had to struggle and meet unpredictable and unprecedented challenges in its short history. But eventually, the growing church's perseverance would be rewarded and the spirit of the early Aglipayan church would be renewed.

Questions for Discussion

1. Geographically and demographically, the UUCP is unlike any other UU context familiar to most. How has their environment helped shaped them? Would there be a parallel equivalent in the North Atlantic UU experience?

2. The "free and responsible search for truth and meaning" is often captured in the journey that many UUs tell—these personal stories become "sacred texts" for

some. How do you respond to the story or "sacred text" of Toribio Quimada?

3. The Universalists responded to "The Philippines Calling." The Unitarians did not. Why might this have been the case?

Rev. Quimada after his college graduation in 1965.

Rev. Quimada accompanying worship with his guitar in Nagbinlod, Santa Catalina, Negros Oriental.

Rev. Quimada receiving the Albert Schweitzer Award for Distinguished Service during the IARF Congress in Tokyo, Japan, 1984.

The charred remains of Rev. Quimada the day after his murder. His wife (on the left), is touching his head as his body lay on a banana leaf.

Chapter 4

Unitarian Universalism in the Philippines

> It was my recognition that the Filipino church had
> been in some sense abandoned by the American-based
> denomination after the Universalists had helped initi-
> ate it [therefore] I became determined to see that the
> church was offered full membership in the UUA.
>
> —William F. Schulz

In 1985, the Universalist Church of the Philippines
changed its name to the Unitarian Universalist Church of
the Philippines, primarily because the Philippine government would not recognize communication between the
UUA and the UCP—the government said that to show a
relationship they had to share a common name. But the
UUCP had wanted a stronger connection than name only:
they wished to be a member of the UUA. This desire was
years old, but the UUA bylaws reserved membership to
"societies, which are located primarily in the United
States and Canada. . . . " (Article III, Section C-3.1) While
not identical, these circumstances recall an earlier situation: in 1936 the Independent Church had the support of
UUA President Cornish, among whose reasons for want-
ing the AUA to promote Aglipay's movement was liberal
religion's unique message and sense of justice. Rebecca
Quimada Sienes quotes from UUA President Schulz who,
sounding like his internationally minded predecessor
Louis Cornish, wrote in *Finding Time & Other Delicacies*:
"One of the measures of our seriousness as a religious
movement is the extent to which we cast our glance be-

yond our own ecclesiastical doors and outside the boundaries of North America. . . . I am convinced that the message we bring—news of a loving God, a responsible
humanity, a liberating faith; support for those who would
break the chains of racism, poverty, and oppression; con-
fidence that the universe extends its arms to us in kind
embrace; assurance that death does not rob life of its
nectar—I am convinced these messages strike a universal chord." (Schulz 1992)

Schulz and UUA Moderator Natalie Gulbrandsen
championed the UUCP's drive to become a member of the
Association—they urged changing the bylaws and elimi-
nating the North American exclusiveness of the Association. Schulz wrote Sienes: "Certainly the fact that your
father had labored with such energy and devotion for so
many years on behalf of our faith impressed me greatly
and I saw the offering of the UUA membership as a way
to repair an injustice. . . . When I became fully aware
(through correspondence with your father) of the history
of the UU Church of the Philippines and of the Church's
sincere desire to become a member of the UUA, I under-
took the push for the change in the Bylaws which would
eliminate the restriction on UUA membership to North
American congregations or expatriate congregations."
(Private correspondence)

A month following Rev. Quimada's murder, at the
UUA General Assembly in Palm Springs, the association's
bylaws were changed and the UUCP was accepted as a
member of the UUA. Rebecca Quimada Sienes, with her
husband Perfecto, attended the assembly and watched as
her father's dream became a reality. It was not an uncon-
tested motion: there were those who opposed—and continue to oppose—opening membership in the UUA to
congregations outside of North America. But the window
had been opened just enough for the UUCP (and others)
to slide in before being closed again. Concerns about cultural differences, religious imperialism, economic disparities, and other issues were raised as reasons to oppose
the measure, and still remain troubling for some.

In November 1988, the UUCP convened a special convention to address the issues that had been raised during the previous tumultuous six months. Leaderless, the main issue on the convention's agenda was the election of a UUCP president. Toribio Quimada's son-in-law, Perfecto Sienes, who had been a student at Silliman and attended Quimada's midweek discussions on religion, was elected. Another significant decision made by the Convention was to move the UUCP office from Nagbinlod to Dumaguete City—home to Silliman University and the provincial airport and easily accessible to all congregations by bus and motorcab.

Not long after UUCP headquarters was moved to Dumaguete, and with support and assistance from Rev. Melvin Hoover of the UUA and Rev. Richard Boeke from the Unitarian Universalist Church of Berkeley (Calif.), an academic relationship was reestablished with the Silliman University Divinity School. Since this reconnection, the UUCP has had students enrolled in the SUDS bachelor of divinity program. In March 1994, degrees were awarded to two UUCP students: Henry Legaje and Pere Carl Quimada Sienes (grandson of Toribio Quimada). This was a grand day! They became the first professional UU ordained ministers in the Philippines, but not the last: the following year Richard Patrivo and Eddie Espartero were graduated and ordained; in June 1999, after three years of study in Chicago and completion of her studies in Dumaguete City, Rebecca Quimada Sienes was awarded her degree from Meadville/Lombard Theological School, becoming the first Filipino UU to receive the master of divinity degree as well as the first ordained woman in the UUCP. * The UU students at SUDS are considered

---

* Sienes was awarded her degree in absentia. It was conferred on her by Ken Maclean, special assistant to UUA President John Buehrens, during the 1999 UUCP Annual Convention in Dumaguete. In completing her studies at SUDS, Rebecca broke new ground: Not only did she become the first Unitarian Universalist student to complete an M.Div. program, but she became the first SUDS student to do community ministry for an internship. Rebecca chose to work with the Marina Clinic—a health clinic that serves the poor and receives some

among the hardest working, brightest, and most outspoken—and there are more to come.

The ten years following Toribio Quimada's death were
full ones. With many mourning the loss of their founder
and good friend and as the Church was challenged by a
variety of issues—charismatic but not always committed
leadership, well-intentioned and struggling programs,
church restructuring and the implementation of guide-
lines for lay leaders and ministers, fund-raising, international participation, serving the needs of poor farming
families—Rebecca Quimada Sienes stepped forward to
carry on her father's dream as well as to share her commitment to and vision of the Unitarian Universalist Principles and Purposes. Elected UUCP president in 1996, she
is dedicated, hard-working, bright, and zealous about
spreading the Unitarian Universalist gospel. She wrote:
"[Unitarian] Universalism in the Philippines is a minority theology in the midst of Roman Catholicism. It is a minority faith among the minority. The late Rev. Quimada
planted the seed of Universalism and it is growing. But,
it is 'growing in pain.' It's up to the present generation of
[Unitarian] Universalists to take good care and nourish
the growing seed. Being the daughter and a witness to the
hard labors of my father in spreading the message of Universalism in the Philippines, I cannot conceive in the remotest corner of my mind that the seed 'growing in pain'
will die. I cannot imagine that the faith he died so violently defending will be forgotten, unremembered, and
neglected in the minds of Unitarians and Universalists in
the rest of the world."

UUCP Organization

The purpose of the UUCP is stated in its Constitution
and Bylaws:

---

funding from the IARF—where she ministered to "domestic sex work-
ers" (DSW), prostitutes, and their families. This included, at her initiative, writing and teaching a Sunday school curriculum for DSW
children.

> The Unitarian Univeralist Church of the Philippines,
> Inc., shall devote its resources and exercise its corporate
> powers for religious, educational and humanitarian pur-
> poses. The church shall help its members uplift their eco-
> nomic lives; strengthen their relationships with one
> another and to the One whom they pay deep homage. It
> shall encourage her members to express freely their beliefs,
> opinions, and views, to use the democratic process in every
> undertaking, and to work for a better world to live with
> peace, liberty, and justice for all, with respect of all exis-
> tence of which we are a part. (Art. III, Sec. 2)

There are twenty-six congregations in the Unitarian
Universalist Church of the Philippines. All but one are
located in rural, mountain, and seacoast *barangays* whose
members are peasant laborers (see appendix 4). Some of
these congregations came with Rev. Quimada from *Iglesia
Universal de Cristo*. None of the congregations has more
than sixty adult members. Except for the building in Dumaguete, which also houses the UUCP office following the
move from Nagbinlod, nearly all the churches are simple
structures: dirt floor, benches or chairs, an altar area with
a UUCP banner, chalice, and centering bell (given by the
UUCP office), and often a blackboard for "lectures,"
classes, or meetings. The structures are usually built by
members with bamboo or other indigenous wood. The
Dumaguete building was a private residence purchased
with money from the UUA in 1988. With several bed-
rooms, kitchen, bathrooms, large meeting areas and a
large yard, it has been a home to UU families and students living in the provincial capital and the site of the
annual convention.

As set out in its Constitution and Bylaws (see appendix 3), there are six elected officers of the UUCP, each
serving a four-year term (for no more than three terms).
The board of directors conducts the business of the
church. The UUCP board consists of the officers (minus
the moderator), committee and organization representatives, and a director-at-large. Organizations include the
Ministers Association, the Women's Association, the

Youth Organization, and the Unitarian Universalist Faith Healers Association of the Philippines. The annual convention is held every April 22–27 (always with a birthday celebration in memory of Rev. Toribio Quimada). In addition to setting overall policy, the convention time is spent in workshops, lectures, worship, and fun. While the leadership and ministers see each other several times during a year, for most of the delegates this is the only time they have to see and talk with each other. Consequently, the convention is like a large family reunion/homecoming and is anticipated all year.

UUCP Ministry

As set forth in the UUCP Constitution and Bylaws, "The ordained religious leaders of the Church shall be the Minister, the Elder, and the Deacon or Deaconess." (Art. X, Sec. 3) An ordained minister's role is stipulated as: "He/she shall be responsible in nurturing its parishioners as to their role in the ministry, preach and teach Unitarianism and Universalism, its principles, the Bible, and the other sacred religious writings that can be used as a guide for ethical living, serve the community by comforting those in sorrow and pain, visiting the sick and the prisoners, helping uplift the spirit of the oppressed and the needy, conduct and perform worship services. He/she may represent his/her congregation or fellowship at special occasions and lead in promoting its welfare." (Art. X., Sec. 3, Para. 1)

Both the elder and deacon/deaconess assist the minister in Sunday and midweek worship, administration, pastoral care, education programs, and any additional duties the minister feels are appropriate.

While congregational polity is observed, which includes the congregation's ordination of any person as minister, elder, or deacon/deaconess, there are "Conditions for Ordination" consisting of knowledge of Unitarian Universalism, leadership skills, active membership in a UUCP congregation, and approval by the UUCP Ministers Association and/or Board of Directors. (Art. X., Sec. 4., Para 1)

An individual must be an ordained minister and meet additional conditions in order to qualify to officiate marriages, which also requires authorization by the Philippine government. In other words, only at the recommendation of the UUCP Ministers Association and the approval of the UUCP Convention Assembly can an ordained minister apply to the government for authority to officiate marriage ceremonies.

All but five UUCP ministers are ordained lay ministers. Only a few are compensated as full-time ministers—and these must be approved by the Convention Assembly. Nearly all perform their ministry in addition to full-time work, usually farming or fishing.* Though members of a congregation see each other all week long, especially in a *barangay,* and often participate in some church function during the week, like mid-week (Wednesday) service, Sunday morning worship is the highlight. The UUCP recommends the following order of worship for its congregations:

Community concerns

Prelude

Lighting of the chalice

Ringing of the bell

Call to worship

Opening hymn

Opening prayer

Responsive reading

---

* There are exceptions, of course. One part-time lay minister teaches high school. Two of the Silliman Divinity School graduates are active in the UUCP, but have had to turn to work other than full-time ministry in order to sustain their income. Rebecca Quimada Sienes receives a salary as president of the UUCP (which is equivalent to being a district minister) and occasionally preaches in area UU congregations.

Pastoral/intercessory prayer

Scripture/Poem reading

Message through a song

Reflection/sermon

Reading

Song

Offering

Prayer of thanks/committal

Closing hymn

Closing prayer

Doxology

Benediction

Healing

Handshake of Peace with song

No congregation has a piano; at least one has an electric keyboard. They all have guitars and there are many who enjoy playing them. Guitar is the preferred instrument of the Philippines, especially in the *barangays*. I was told by Divinity School students that guitar playing is required for graduation—a necessary reality when they are called to *barangay* churches. Many of the hymns sung in UUCP congregations are traditional Filipino Christian folk hymns that most have heard since childhood (church members delight in singing these and will sing them slowly, drawn out with five and six verses). As a way of introducing Unitarian Universalist hymns, responsive readings, and the UU Principles and Purposes, Rebecca Quimada Sienes, with grant money from the UUA, published two hymnals for the UUCP—one in Cebuano, the other in Hiligaynon. Slowly these are being accepted by the congregations as an integral part of worship.

The UUCP hymnal reflects the UU Christian theology that is characteristic of its members. Liberal in its Catholic context, it's similar to the UU Christianity found among many North Atlantic UU Christians. But the theology-shaping influences that produced this belief are unique to the UUs of Negros, different from any western UU context.

Questions for Discussion

1. Regarding his support of the UUCP's membership in the UUA, President William Schulz wrote: "One of the measures of our seriousness as a religious movement is the extent to which we cast our glance beyond our own ecclesiastical doors and outside the boundaries of North America." What is your reaction to this statement?

2. "[Unitarian Universalism in the Philippines] is a minority faith among the minority," says Rebecca Quimada Sienes. Catholicism has always been the dominant faith community in the archipelago. In this context, do you think there would be unique pressures on a member of the UUCP? Might there be any equivalent to this in the North Atlantic UU community?

3. Look through the UUCP Constitution and Bylaws in appendix 3. Is there anything that strikes you as different or unusual?

Ang Sulondan Sang Pagsimba

Mga Kalantahon, Pagtolon-an, kag mga Kamatouran

Sang Iglesia

Unitarian Universalist of the Philippines
National Office
065 Rovira Road, Bantayan
6200 Dumaguete City, Negros Oriental
Philippines

UUCP hymnal cover

Members of the Banaybanay, Bayawan, Negros Oriental UU congregation in their church. On the far right is Rev. Toribio Cortez.

Susan, a member of the Banaybanay church, and some children in front of a home.

Sunday morning worship with lay participation at the UU Church of Banaybanay.

The congregation at Kalumboyan, Bayawan, Negros Oriental.

Chapter 5

Theology and the Unitarian Universalist Church of the Philippines

There is only one God who is the God of love.

—UUCP Principles

On the hour-long plane trip from Manila to Dumaguete City, I had with me a draft of amendments and suggestions to the UUCP Constitution and Bylaws from Rev. Pere Carl Q. Sienes. He had asked me to review them before I reached Negros then discuss them with his mother, Rev. Rebecca Quimada Sienes, before they were given to the UUCP Board of Directors. They all appeared routine until I turned one page and read the title of a UUCP organization: "The Unitarian Universalist Faith Healers Association of the Philippines." My curiosity piqued, I looked ahead to locate a mention of the group in the Association's Constitution and Bylaws, which I found in the appendices—but it was written in Cebuano. I would have to wait several days before I would get a translation.

Faith healing is just one of the dramatic differences a western Unitarian Universalist will find while visiting the UUCP on Negros—there are not only changes in climate, culture, and style, but significant differences in liberal theology. In some respects, Louis Cornish's observations and veiled plea for insight, respect, and understanding are as relevant today as they were in 1936: "Perhaps some day the sons of men will have the grace to comprehend that the Mass and the Quaker Meeting, and all the ways of public worship which resemble the one or the other, are to be judged not by their appearance but by their teachings; and that all who love God and their fellow-men, whatever be their form of worship, may be truly part of God's Holy and Catholic and Universal Church of the aspiring mind and the understanding heart." (1942, 100) Cornish was saying then, and it could apply today as well, Don't judge the Philippine liberal church or rush to complain about its theology and practices based on initial impressions: experience and learn about it, be open to them.

All theology, regardless of the era, is shaped by personal and social factors. Filipino UU theology is no different. There are five influences shaping this theology— influences that are penetrating, pervasive, and lasting as well as interdependent. These are Roman Catholicism, oppression, independent Protestantism, faith healing, and an absence of a common heritage. Each has roots in the others so that when one is tugged another is nudged too. Let's look at each of these influences.

Roman Catholicism is the essence of Filipino life. From the crucifixes in provincial offices to the week of special Easter television and radio shows that coup all other programming; from the Philippine Senate president's five-minute prime-time television message urging Filipinos to observe the lessons of Jesus Christ and shape a better nation to bus divers who cross themselves every time they reenter and start their bus; from the small Roman Catholic churches that are found in nearly every *barangay* to the television stations that go off the air in observance of Holy Week; from the newspaper's editorial page worship box to Roman Catholic relics in courtrooms—the nation is steeped in the Roman Catholic tradition. Likewise, even among the most committed Unitarian Universalists, Catholicism is part of their religious routine: following a funeral conducted by a UUCP minister, the *barangay* residents traveled for forty-five minutes—to the closest Catholic church—for a one-hour mass; a Sunday congregation recites prayers and unison and responsive readings in a fast-paced, rote style similar to mass; members want to know if it is okay to believe that Jesus is God, to pray in the name of the Trinity, and to read the Bible. From the most overt ways to the most subtle, Roman Catholicism is part of Philippine life—this is the accepted reality. More than this, really: Roman Catholicism is as natural and everyday to Philippine culture as are breathing, eating, and sleeping to life—Filipinos don't even think about it. What Cornish wrote decades ago still describes today: "During more than three centuries these [Roman Catholic] forms have been part of the warp and woof of Filipino life." (1942, 98) Virtually everyone participates in the Catholic culture in some way—just living in the Philippines means participating.

As a result of Roman Catholicism's penetrating and pervasive impact, Unitarian Universalists bring to their congregations a potpourri of expectations, history, and beliefs that wouldn't ordinarily be found in most Unitarian Universalist contexts. Creedalistic rather than covenantal, ritualistic and formulaic in worship, the UUCP is liberal Christianity not so much as an Aglipayan version—which was very Roman Catholic in appearance (a point made by Cornish). With its rigid dogma, punitive social theology, and authoritarian past, Roman Catholicism has contributed to the oppressive experience of all Filipinos.

Interdependent with Catholicism, conditions created by the government and poverty are additional oppressions under which all Unitarian Universalists (and most Filipinos) must live. In spite of the greatly heralded "People's Revolution" resulting in the election of Cory Aquino in 1986, the vestiges of terror, uncertainty, and insecurity from decades of authoritarian rule, especially under Ferdinand Marcos, continue. Many never returned to their land after relocation was completed in the name of national security; some who disappeared were never found; university and seminary faculty who lost their positions because they dared to speak out for academic freedom were never reinstated; the risks can still be tremendous for anyone—poor farmer, teacher, or lawyer—who is left-of-conservative in their politics. People continue to be reluctant to speak their minds— they are reluctant to put their faith into action; the recent past still surrounds them, close enough to keep them in check. In the *barangay* of Nagbinlod, a kilometer outside of town, is a small garrison that houses a unit of the Philippine Special Forces, who make regular patrols through the mountains and jungle. "We occasionally hear gun-fire and have reports of ongoing insurgent activity," the commanding sergeant told me. "Our work is not complete." Nagbinlod is where Rev. Toribio Quimada was murdered. In Caican, I overheard several wives tell others that their husbands wouldn't be joining the Sunday festivities: their men were "asked" to participate in cleaning and restoring the Santa Catalina garrison. This was said in a sarcastic, eye-rolling manner, as if to suggest that the military was simply using this as an excuse to remind *barangay* residents of their presence. Neither of these instances poses a direct threat to villagers, but they are daily reminders of who's in charge, reminders that people are being watched, reminders that the government is ever-present.

Being a minority (Unitarian Universalist) in a minority (Protestantism), Unitarian Universalism is unheard of, and even though it's Christian—albeit liberal Christian— it is suspect. While members of the UUCP don't feel they need to hide their religion, neither are they willing to draw attention to their faith community. They won't use the word *liberal* to describe their faith, since *liberal* carries a highly charged negative political meaning for most; UUCPers are reluctant to talk about or use the word *humanism* for the same reason; some Unitarian Universalists are cautious about referring to their faith community's welcoming spirit to all religions since, for example, Muslims on Mindanao (and reportedly on Negros) regularly challenge the government with acts of disruption. The oppressive leadership and policies that dictated life in the Philippines for centuries—the recent memory of Toribio Quimada's murder and the likelihood that there will be no justice—signal and remind Unitarian Universalists that they must be careful, live cautiously, and stay within the status quo.

The oppression experienced by Unitarian Universalists is not only from government constraints but from abject poverty. The Philippines is a nation of people who live with a kind of material poverty unparalleled in the United States (or in the North Atlantic)—a kind of poverty so foreign to the West that words and pictures cannot convey its character and effect. The Unitarian Universalist Church of the Philippines is a church of the poor—the poor peasant class (as opposed to the urban poor as seen in Manila). Like other peasant poor, they live in small homes of bamboo (or other indigenous wood) that are shared with their children and extended family members. Rice is the mainstay of their diet along with dried fish, vegetables, and fruit. Most women stay at home to tend to domestic chores and most men work in the sugarcane fields, rice paddies or, if on the coast, they fish. (As noted earlier, there are very few UUs who are not peasant poor—I could count them on two hands.)

Peasant life in a coastal or mountain *barangay* is simple by western twenty-first-century expectations—comparable to small-town rural life in the United States 200 years ago. The day begins before sunrise (4:30–5:00) and ends at sunset (most *barangays* don't have electricity). Children attend the local elementary school but high school is optional, especially since distance is often prohibitive; public high schools are regional and closer private schools charge tuition. A highlight on any day is when a *jeepney* (a public bus that serves a *barangay*) comes through with passengers and cargo. Chickens, cattle, and dogs wander the one or two roads and countless paths, none of which are lighted at night, which necessitates starting home at dusk to avoid wandering off the trail or stepping in the holes and ruts that mark all the mountain roads. Following a light rain, roads can be washed out, and after a heavy rain, *barangays* can be unreachable for days. Cooking in a *barangay* home is over open fires, though many homes also have an outdoor cooking area especially for preparing poultry or beef (that is, larger foods).

None of these conditions or characteristics is particular to Unitarian Universalists; they are shared by everyone in a *barangay*. What is unique to Unitarian Universalism on Negros is that these are the conditions of nearly all UUs. Unlike in other Protestant faith communities, there are no middle-class or wealthy UUCP congregations or members. In a similar vein, *barangay* residents, I was told, are looked down on by those living in towns or cities because rural people look, walk, and talk differently; their ways visibly set them apart from others—they're considered "backward." Again, this is life in a *barangay,* nothing unique to Unitarian Universalism. But when you are a UU (a minority within a minority) and poor and from a *barangay,* this "triple whammy" can be an obstacle. Like being a member of the UUCP, a Unitarian Universalist in the United States means being from a tiny and misunderstood faith community. But dissimilar to Unitarian Universalism on Negros, U.S. Unitarian Universalists are recognized and accepted by most as "mainline" with a deep and prestigious heritage, as well as having abundant membership resources.

A third shaping influence on members of the UUCP is the independence of the Protestant spirit. For most Filipinos, Protestantism is something new and bold—an untried way in uncharted territory. In some respects, Protestantism is not only independent from but a protest against both Roman Catholicism and government, which are often seen and felt as one. This merging of church and state in the aftermath of Iberian colonial rule—even a hundred years later—is not unique to the Philippines. Writing for the *Atlantic Monthly,* Francis Fukuyama commented: "The imperial and Latin Catholic traditions of Spain and Portugal reinforced dependence on large, centralized institutions like the State and the Church, weakening an independent civil society." (1999, 59) As we have already seen, the oppressive roles of government and poverty and the centralized nature of both leave no one untouched: the government and poverty are everywhere, permeating even the most geographically protected and remote areas.

Since 1898 the Protestant spirit has challenged this centralized control of church and state by empowering, albeit not all in the same way, individuals and congregations—especially in those faith communities, like Unitarian Universalism, where there is a strong emphasis on and expression of individual freedom of belief and congregational polity. Both of these, given the "dependence on large, centralized institutions," pose a significant shift from the historical and everyday, which, of course, is part of its appeal. Though I experienced the Protestant spirit in many ways, one example will suffice.

On a hot, humid Sunday afternoon, fifty members of the Banaybanay congregation turned out to listen to and participate in a two-hour talk I gave on the Bible. Their interest in the subject was reflected in the questions and concerns they raised throughout the presentation. About halfway through I could see a young couple returning from church—in the distance I saw them leave the village Pentecostal church and make their way on the path toward the UU church. They entered their traditional *barangay* home directly across from the church entrance. Within moments, they were sitting in their window, listening to the talk and discussion. It wasn't long before they wandered into the presentation, sitting in the back. After ten minutes they shared this: what they knew about the Bible they learned from others since neither of them could read. What they were hearing in this congregation's discussion—in my talk—was new to them, unlike anything they had heard before. Both wanted to learn more. Several in the Banaybanay congregation talked with them about their UU congregation, and not long after the man asked by what authority we spoke about such things: Tell me more about who you are, he was asking.

The visit from this couple and the insights, beliefs, and explanations we discussed regarding the differences between creedal and covenantal religion dramatize the significance of the Unitarian Universalist presence in Filipino life. For centuries Filipinos have been told by the Church and government what to do and what to believe. The freedom to believe and the independence of volunteer association—religious freedoms they have had for more than 100 years—are still, for many, novel ideas and ones difficult to conceive and practice because they go against all the experiences they have had up until now, experiences handed down for generations. Just as many U.S. Unitarian Universalists speak about the refreshing and rejuvenating experiences they have with their congregations after finding a supportive UU faith community, Filipino Unitarian Universalists—as well as Protestants in general—speak about the joy and energy they feel due to congregational polity and freedom of belief. In large part, these have been due to the Protestant spirit ushered in after the Spanish-American War.

The interrelating influences of Catholicism, oppression, and the Protestant spirit are all embodied and find expression in the fourth shaping factor: faith healing. Faith healing is about empowerment, independence, and protest, and it provides an authentic substitute to modern medicine. Faith healing is a religious and social phenomenon by which many UUCP members find Unitarian Universalism appealing and sustaining. At least half of UUCP ministers practice faith healing as do some lay people, while virtually all Unitarian Universalists in the Philippines believe in it.

The Unitarian Universalist Faith Healers Association of the Philippines (UUFHA), open to all UUCP ministers, states in the preamble of its Bylaws: "We unite ourselves to study and heal the sick persons through prayer in faith to God. This requires compassion to all members that need help." * Under its Principles and Policies it explains: "This Association is a group that heals all equally, with

* While the purpose of the UUFHA is compassion, it must also prevent the practice of harmful ways, misuses of the healing gift. For example, in Article 10, Association Prohibitions, there are two provisions: "1. A

justice. The power is pure, coming from God and from the Lord Jesus Christ when sick people believe they can be healed through prayer to God and Jesus Christ." At least once a year, members of the UUFHA gather for a retreat at which they share experiences and lend support and nurturing to each others' ministry. Their faith healing is not restricted to the members of their congregations. In fact, many become Unitarian Universalist as a result of being healed—as a result of the healing and charismatic leadership. Though healing is included in the suggested order of service (see Art. X, Sec. 2. of the UUCP Constitution and Bylaws in appendix 3), the number of people seeking to be healed is often so many—and healing is so time-consuming—that some congregations practice the healing before and after the service, even concurrent with the Sunday service.

There are at least three reasons for the existence of UU faith healing in the Philippines. First, it is indigenous—faith healing is a thread in the fabric of Philippine tradition and culture, and has been for thousands of years. Second, faith healing is merely one of the many ways that the Philippine world is alive: whether in spirits, dreams, the earth, animals, or ancestors, everything about life is animated and can be manipulated, interacted with, learned from. And third, the forces and insights that are outside the realm of human creation often can be, by the right person in the right context, used for the health and well-being of individuals.

The Philippine government recognized the role and value of these indigenous beliefs and practices by enacting The Traditional and Alternative Medicine Act (TAMA) of 1997 (Republic Act No. 8423). Not only did this legisla-

---

member is not allowed to use his/her healing wisdom/power to compete with another faith healer. 2. Every member is prohibited to use his/her power to practice *paghaladhalad sa maga diwatahan.*" This "practice" consists of chopping up a pure white or black chicken and spreading the pieces under a tree for the spirits to consume, thereby placing an evil hex on another. This is considered against the law of God.

tion give legitimacy to ancient, traditional Philippine practices, but it also relieved the growing threat of malpractice lawsuits that were being filed against traditional praticioners, a fear, concern, and challenge that could have had disturbing and far-reaching consequences if it had not been addressed. For example, prior to this legislation, many practioners of traditional remedies sought the protection and refuge of the church in order to continue practicing their beliefs. Very few churches wanted to acknowledge indigenous remedies, viewing them as superstitious, harmful, and contrary to Christian faith—even though leadership acknowledged the everyday use and deep cultural roots of these practices.

For Christians, especially, their opposition posed a slight contradiction, since many faith healers grounded their practice in James 5:14–15: "Are any among you sick? They should call for the elders of the church and have them pray over them, anointing them with oil in the name of the Lord. The prayer of faith will save the sick, and the Lord will raise them up; and anyone who has committed sins will be forgiven." Rebecca Quimada Sienes writes: "From its inception, faith healing has been an event in our church that is widely practiced. In the olden days of the church, at the end of the Sunday Service, church leaders and ministers would come up to the pulpit and lay their hands on the sick persons and offer a healing prayer. The Church does not subscribe to a particular practice, however ministers, church leaders or members who would like to engage in such practice are given the liberty to do so. There are those who are practicing faith healing, herbal healing, and divine healing." (1994b, 29)

In the UUCP, some ministers (and the congregants who followed them), in order to practice their faith healing, took sanctuary in Unitarian Universalism's freedom and tolerance of belief; Unitarian Universalism was a theologically inclusive faith community that supported not only their beliefs but their right to these beliefs, thereby shielding them from the government and the Church. With the passage of TAMA, the fear of government persecution diminished, though the denial and discouraging rhetoric of the orthodox church remains unchanged.

For many western Unitarian Universalists, as for many professional ministers (i.e., seminary graduates), the practice of faith healing is a perplexing and confusing, if not troubling, phenomenon: faith healing appears to be contrary to everything we have been taught and experienced in Unitarian Universalism. Rebecca Sienes provides some clarity by explaining: "If one is a minister or perhaps a church leader in a society where medical services are expensive, scarce, and remote it is to the advantage of the minister to know beyond what the church theologies say, how to fully address all the people's needs. On the part of the healer, it means a holy connection with the mystery and the power of the Supreme Being and its evolving truth. While to poor, sick persons for whom medical services are expensive, faith healing means salvation." (1994b, 29)

This might begin to explain the "why" to a questioning mind, but what about the "how"? I was further confused after a conversation with two UUCP ministers, both graduates of seminary. We were talking about the prevalence of faith healing in UUCP congregations—both of them were sharing their distrust of it, saying they didn't believe in it and hoping that there would be a change in the future. Both related experiences where they had been accused by ordained lay ministers and congregants of being "hard-headed," doubters of the power, closed to the Biblical basis for faith healing. Yet, without any recognition of contradiction, each shared about the several times they had sought out the comfort, advice and power of faith healers! Why not? they admitted—after all, it has worked for so many!

There is something more going on here than the curing of physical infirmity. I'll share two examples. Rachel had done something that angered her husband. In revenge, he placed a hex on her that caused her to break out with a very unsightly rash. She was embarrassed by it, thinking that others now knew about her domestic troubles. She went several times to the medical center for treatment and found no relief. Finally she went to several Unitarian Universalist faith healers. Weeks after, she started to heal.

Clara had suffered physical and verbal abuse from her husband. She developed headaches a week after a certain incident and went to her Unitarian Universalist minister. She had been receiving a laying on of hands weekly from him for a month.

Both of these women could in fact have an organic cause to their distress. But there is also a social aspect. John Dominic Crossan provides insight in his examination of healing among the poor—among the powerless and disenfranchised, such as those who were visited by Jesus. Crossan draws a distinction between disease and illness that is helpful: "A *disease* is, to put it bluntly, between me, my doctor, and a bug. Something is wrong with my body, and I take it to a doctor to be fixed. What is lacking in that picture is not just the entire psychological but, much more important, the entire social dimension of the phenomenon. How have I been trained to think of my body, modern medicine, and doctors? How does my dysfunction involve my family, my job, or, in some cases, wider and wider levels of society? *Disease* sees the problem, unrealistically, on the minimal level; *illness*, realistically, on the wider level. Think, for example, of the difference between curing the disease or healing the illness known as AIDS. A cure for the disease is absolutely desirable, but in its absence, we can still heal the illness by refusing to ostracize those who have it, by empathizing with their anguish, and by enveloping their sufferings with both respect and love." (1994, 81)

Crossan's analysis doesn't explain everything—I don't want to explain everything! But for members of North Atlantic culture, and for Unitarian Universalists, Crossan provides a place for followers of liberal religion to start coming to grips with a phenomenon very unlike anything in our realm of experience and belief, yet integral to the practice and belief of liberal religion in the Philippines. I believe the only way to completely and fully understand and appreciate the practice and receiving of faith-healing—as well as other traditional healing remedies—is to be a member of Philippine culture. To have grown up with it and come to expect it are something quite different from observing it from outside the culture.

Finally, faith healing and other traditional, indigenous remedies are the closest thing that Unitarian Universalists have to a shared, national heritage. The absence of a deep, common Filipino cultural tradition is the fifth theology-shaping influence among Unitarian Universalists on Negros. Karnow's summary, "Three centuries in a Catholic convent and fifty years in Hollywood," reflects this void. Prior to Spanish colonialism, there were Chinese and Southeast Asian influences which may be seen in the physical traits of Filipinos; there are customs that many practice, observe, and celebrate every year, customs that are described as Filipino traditions; some foods share a common recognition among many as unique to a region; there are songs, instruments, dances, and clothes that many describe as Filipino. Yet, these are not defining characteristics or attributes of Filipinos—these are not theology-shaping factors for Unitarian Universalists (or any other Filipinos). Contrasting this condition will help to clarify it.

Recently, my wife and I were having a meal with a Russian public school teacher—a colleague that my wife had visited during an exchange program. The Russian was describing the plight of her fellow citizens as they tried to cope with an unstable economy, unpredictable leadership, an irrelevant church, and changing values. Everything she named I had heard described and seen on Negros—maybe even more extreme conditions. Yet there was an underlying resolve and feistiness in her voice; a pride, outrage, determination, and perseverance that I never heard from any Filipino. On Negros, what I heard and saw among so many was resignation and acceptance.

What was the difference? There are probably explanations I can't fathom. But what is clear is that Russians are a proud people who share an ancient social and cultural heritage that is recognized worldwide. And more importantly, it's a heritage that many Russians find of tremendous value: they may be frustrated, confused, and threatened by their current experiences, but they have a common history that allows them to transcend some of the daily insults and keep hoping and working for a better Russia. I did not experience this pride or resolve on Negros. The continuing and defining influences of Spanish colonial Catholicism, the oppressions of government and poverty, and the importation of the Protestant spirit are a few of the signs that reflect this bankruptcy of a shared heritage. Stated another way, the heritage that is shared by so many is not an uplifting, empowering, or motivating heritage. Luis H. Francia writes: "In the Philippine context, what is foreign and what is indigenous has always been a tricky and ultimately impossible subject. For better or worse, Filipinos have unconsciously perfected the art of mixing the two up, confounding definitions and scholars." (1993, xiii) Francia goes on to provide a wonderful summarizing metaphor of this challenge: "Imagine an American-made train, its luggage racks and boxcars crammed with American baggage and freight. Imagine the train rolling out of the depot and across the country; picking up Filipino passengers along the way. As the train's racks and freight cars are filled with what to the Filipino are strange-looking suitcases, portmanteaus, and various other items, it becomes readily apparent that there is no place for his or her own luggage. In a supreme act of accommodation, many chuck their goods out the window and cheerfully appropriate what is already there. But as the train goes deeper and deeper into the countryside, more and more passengers come aboard until eventually one or two or three start to toss out the strange-looking suitcases, portmanteaus, and various other items and replace them with their own, but made of bamboo, rattan, buri. And almost everyone follows suit, until finally the

train's metamorphosis is complete, and it becomes indis-
putably Philippine." (Ibid., xv)

After centuries of colonial and imperialist rule, there
is no telling where the Philippines will come out culturally. Spanish and U.S. wounds are deep and the scars are
many. The absence of a clear and shared heritage has left
its mark on UU theology. Catholicism, oppression, the
Protestant spirit, faith healing, and an absence of a common heritage—these five factors have shaped UUCP theology and ecclesiology.

Given these five influences, it isn't surprising to see
the faith they have shaped. The Sunday and midweek services are highly predictable, structured, liturgical, and
full of ritual—everything one might expect in such an
overwhelmingly Catholic culture. To ask members of a
Unitarian Universalist church why they worship in the
manner they do is to invite looks and expressions of confusion or disbelief, as if to say, "There is another way?" For
nearly all Unitarian Universalists, their very structured
Sunday and midweek order and bible-centered worship is
what they know—and is all they have known.

And it is a biblical faith—theocentric with the role of
Jesus central to their lives: Jesus is a religious, ethical, social, and political figure of profound importance. UUCP
members are open to other faiths, to a diversity of belief,
they welcome the insights and challenges posed by those
outside of their faith community (and from those inside it
too). But there is no doubt that the UUCP is Christian.
They are (William Ellery) Channing Unitarians in their
liberal understanding of Jesus and the value they place
on religious free-thinking. But they are not intellectuals,
and in this sense, and many others, they are remarkably
like Murray Universalists. In *Redeeming Time,* Tim
Jensen has a description of the people evangelized by
John Murray which, with a few name changes, easily fits
the faith and conditions of the UUCP:

> Thomas Potter might well be considered prototypical of
> the kind of person attracted to Universalism—relatively

uneducated, but by no means ignorant, and both curious and vitally concerned about matters of religion. Calvinist doctrines such as double predestination, unconditional election, and limited atonement seemed to contradict an intuitive sense of free will, moral accountability, and the sovereign existence of a benevolent, all-powerful God.

Unlike Unitarianism, Universalism existed outside the establishment. Its congregations tended to be small, rural, and poorly funded; its ministers were either itinerant circuit riders or "tentmakers" who earned part or all of their living by farming or in some other occupation. Many of them began their careers much the same way as the people in the pews, because they found the idea of universal salvation congenial to their own views. Universalists also tended to be uniformly despised as dangerous heretics by orthodox members of the religious establishment, and therefore no strangers to public controversy. (1999, 15)

During my visit I experienced and observed the characteristics described by Jensen. For example, during lectures in several congregations and in adult education classes, people were far more interested and attentive than I anticipated. They were uneducated but by no means ignorant, and were curious and concerned about religious issues. I was often asked to continue. Often the only reason a session came to an end was because we had a travelling schedule to maintain. They asked excellent questions, questions that reflected interest in and thoughtfulness about the topics.

During opportunities of this sort, as well as at ministerial and congregational meetings, at Sunday and midweek worship, and in private conversations, the value they placed on individual freedom and congregational autonomy was accentuated. It was as though after decades of punitive and restrictive rules enforced by the government and church, and in spite of the fact that their peasant life didn't empower them with much authority, in their church and with their beliefs they were in charge—no one could demean, deny, or demand of them while in their Unitarian Universalist context. As a congregation and as members, they were free. Such freedom and flexibility is still unique in the Philippines. While neither church nor state has authority to restrict belief or assembly, the mind-set is such that many just don't think beyond the boundaries that have been in place for centuries. Members of the UUCP are very proud of what they have built and sustain. In their context, the UUCP and what it symbolizes are a beacon and inspiration to many.

What is quite remarkable is that, given the difficult geographic, social, political, and religious conditions under which most Unitarian Universalists live, in spite of the continuing and powerful authoritarian and punitive messages from church and state, in the face of poverty conditions that most from the North Atlantic could not imagine, and given that most people on Negros don't continue their education beyond the elementary level—given these realities, it is remarkable that the message of Universalism originated and grew among the people on the island. Philippine novelist Ninotchka Rosca, in *Twice Blessed* (1992), has a character describe the Filipino mind-set: "[Fear] is the single most powerful constant among the people of this archipelago. We're raised to fear everything: fate, gods, the elements of nature, authority, even joy." Catholicism, oppression, the Protestant spirit of independence, faith healing, and the absence of a shared cultural heritage—these theology-shaping influences all have contributed to and underscored the fear Rosca writes about. Again, the parallel to the conditions and rapid rise and appeal of Universalism in the late-eighteenth-century United States is striking: in the face of hardships on many fronts, the gospel of Universalism thrived. On the island of Negros, for nearly fifty years, in spite of a heritage and conditions that are as far from the Universalist gospel as they can be, they regularly sing: "To teach the hope that is for all, Proclaim the Universal call."

Questions for Discussion

1. In this chapter we read: "All theology is shaped by personal and social factors." Of the five shaping influences

on UUCP theology, which ones do you find most surprising, compelling, challenging? What are equivalent
influences on North Atlantic UU theology?

2. What about the UUCP makes it Unitarian Universalist?

3. Philippine novelist Ninotchka Rosca, in *Twice Blessed*,
has a character describe the Filipino mind-set: "[Fear]
is the most powerful constant among the people of this
archipelago. We're raised to fear everything." Could
this be the reason for Universalism's appeal on Negros?

Rebecca Sienes, third from left, and Rafael Vibar, far right, the minister in Nagbinlod, Santa Catalina, Negros Oriental, along with members
of the Nagbinlod congregation, survey the church's sugarcane field.

UUCP ministers following their Unitarian Universalist Ministers Association meeting.

Chapter 6

The Future of the Unitarian Universalist Church of the Philippines

It's up to the present generation of [Unitarian] Universalists to take good care and nourish the growing seed [of our faith]. Being the daughter and a witness to the hard labors of my father in spreading the message of Universalism in the Philippines, I cannot conceive in the remotest corner of my mind that the seed will die. I cannot imagine that the faith he died so violently defending will be forgotten, unremembered, and neglected in the minds of the Unitarians and Universalists in the rest of the world. The [Unitarian] Universalists in Southeast Asia are not different from the [Unitarian] Universalists in North and South America, Europe, and in other countries.

—Rebecca Quimada Sienes

Under the current leadership of the Rev. Rebecca Quimada Sienes—a Filipina of enormous vision, energy, ability, and commitment—the Unitarian Universalist Church of the Philippines is balancing the challenges it faces, challenges posed by all the issues any faith community will face but, of course, in the Philippine (Negros) context. With support from the Unitarian Universalist Association (and UUA affiliate groups like the International Council of Unitarians and Universalists and the Partner Church Council) and the International Association for Religious Freedom, UUCP leadership works to keep current with the international liberal religious community, leadership opportunities, changing styles of administration and organization, and Philippine current events especially significant to the church. (Silliman University does a great job of extending itself to the UUCP office in Dumaguete City, plus there are always UU students at the University and/or the Divinity School.)

Given the remoteness of most UUCP congregations from the church office and each other, and since communication among congregations is only by letter (and this is totally dependent on the frequency and likelihood of delivery), leadership and organization is not always smooth. It's not uncommon to wait weeks for a response to a letter, to wait days for someone to attend a meeting, and often to hear nothing at all. Rather than sending a letter and waiting for a response, it's not uncommon for a person simply to take a bus across the island or into the mountains, find the person they need to see, conduct their business, and then return on the evening or night bus. In addition, the Philippine bureaucracy is burdensome, slow, and inefficient. Making international travel plans, using the courts, and researching vital statistics, for example, can be arduous if not impossible (unless you "know" someone) for even the educated and urbane—so imagine a rural peasant, minister, or layperson trying to use the system. This is all to say that despite the energy, vision, and commitment to the UUCP of the church's leadership, there are numerous obstacles that challenge even the best and most undaunted of them. Nevertheless, UUCP leaders have overcome many setbacks during the church's brief lifetime, and there is no reason to think that they can't sustain the strong precedents already in place.

In large part, the UUCP's future is resting on the leadership that will follow Rebecca Quimada Sienes and others. Currently, that leadership is its seminary-trained, professional clergy and divinity school students: Rev. Pere Carl Q. Sienes, Rev. Henry S. Legaje, Rev. Richard Patrivo, and Rev. Pablo Quimada; and Silliman Divinity School students Susan Quisel and Elvira Peras Sienes. Like the current leadership, they too are visionaries and are committed to the liberal Christian church on Negros. But the demands on recently ordained ministers and graduates—as in the North Atlantic Unitarian Universalist community—are new and many. Along with their divinity school ecumenical training, UUCP ministers graduate with high expectations of their ministry, the church, and the congregations they will serve. They are dedicated and eager, they are idealistic about the future, they have a gospel to share, and they have time to give. If provided the opportunity, support, encouragement, and resources, they—and those still to come—will respond to the challenges of leadership by sustaining a lighted chalice for future generations of Filipino Unitarian Universalists.

An immediate issue for the future will be growth—of new congregations and resources. The UUCP is, except for one congregation, a rural peasant church: the parallels to the early Universalist Church are striking. As the Universalists eventually took their gospel to the larger towns and then the cities, so too must the UUCP. Remaining a church of the poor will not sustain a robust future for the church—it won't satisfy the emerging leadership. Strengthening the congregation in Dumaguete and starting one in Bacolod City are being discussed. There are religious liberals in these urban settings that have yet to hear the Unitarian Universalist message, and they will respond.

Unlike anything the North Atlantic Unitarian Universalist movement has demonstrated so far, there is the potential for class diversity in the UUCP. There are already several congregations that have limited but committed middle-class leadership. Especially in the more metropolitan areas, a mix of lower and middle classes is not an unrealistic goal, and is one that the current UUCP leadership has embraced. Achieving this goal could provide numerous challenges: in such a small movement, balancing economic extremes could take careful planning and thoughtful attention—a real test of local and island-wide leadership and trust.

The hardships and circumstances faced by most members and congregations of the UUCP—as reflected in the theology-shaping influences of Catholicism, oppression, the Protestant spirit, faith healing, and the lack of a strong Filipino cultural and social heritage—are significant variables in the future of the movement and they are all interrelated. The oppressive and punitive legacies created by the church and state—legacies that have contributed to illiteracy, poverty, class immobility, cronyism, fear, and a widespread reluctance to challenge the status quo—are being addressed, resulting in institutions, behavior, and beliefs that are empowering and liberating, while at the same time unfamiliar and weak, with outcomes including both frustration and abuse. For example, the oppression fostered by the Catholic Church and state has led to an exuberant embracing of personal and institutional religious autonomy. But the move from a heritage of colonial Catholic authoritarianism to a version of American capitalistic democracy has not been a smooth transition (some might argue that it has been a complete failure). So much of what liberal or independent Philippine Protestantism seeks to emulate is rooted in the Western (American) experience and won't translate easily: nothing in Filipino history has prepared Unitarian Universalists for this dramatic shift in paradigms. Another example: Faith healing, like other indigenous, traditional practices, is now recognized by the government, which protects its practitioners, many of whom are Unitarian Universalists. Yet at the same time the legislation gives legitimacy to age-old traditional remedies, it further distances the poor from any hope of modern medical care (it does nothing to bring modern medical care closer to *barangay* peasants and could further distance this possibility). It could also have consequences for the free, liberal church—churches with less formal, less structured ecclesiology—by increasing its susceptibility to charlatans, profiteers, quacks, and the well-intentioned but misguided who are likely to prey on the disenfranchised poor and undereducated living on the edges of the status quo.

In these ways and others, the UUCP's future is challenged by that which is at once its greatest promise (freedom and liberation) as well as its biggest danger (responsibility and caution). There is no swift or easy path for the UUCP to follow, only a journey that is sure to have a myriad of detours and delays, starts and stops.

On this journey, there will be many outside the Philippine context who will provide support, encouragement, and resources. Already, the North Atlantic liberal religious community has been a significant contributor to the UUCP's development. There are important lessons for us to learn from the past fifty years—and before that in the dual role played by Louis Cornish (first as AUA president, then as IALCRF president). First, due primarily to the Philippines' heritage of centralized authority, whereby government and institutions are run and coordinated in hierarchical, top-down fashion, it would be easy for the UUCP to continue this tradition by relying on North Atlantic support in such a way that fosters a dependent paternalism. This would be so easy to do—and in many respects this kind of relationship might even feel natural (and given the Philippines' experience of 350 years of imperialist rule, it would probably feel familiar).

Also, there are North Atlantic organizational and educational opportunities and expectations that may not work for the UUCP. Though colonized by the West, the Philippines is an Asian nation. While western influences can be found in academic institutions, divinity school preparation, and leadership styles as well as in cultural and leisure activities, these often are in glaring contradistinction to the nation's Pacific Rim context and heritage. It will be a challenge for the UUCP to balance North Atlantic expectations (or demands)—whether from the media, government, or supportive parties—with Asian context and customs.

Finally, the UUCP will need to inform, educate, and stretch the imaginations of its brothers and sisters in the North Atlantic liberal religious community, whose vision and version of the Unitarian Universalist faith can be, at times, parochial and exclusive. This will require patience and perseverance, because history demonstrates western colonialism's reluctance to relinquish its claims and influence even after independence and autonomy are won and exercised. North American Unitarian Universalism especially may be quick to assert that the UUCP's theology, organization, and ministry are not Unitarian Universalist at all merely because they don't resemble their American understanding of the liberal, free church. This is the same provincialism encountered by Cornish, Aglipay, and de los Reyes. Cornish wrote about American Unitarians' difficulty in seeing liberal religion in a foreign (Asian) context: "Failure to grasp this fact has caused much misunderstanding about the Philippine Independent Churches. American visitors attending the services conducted in Spanish or one of the native Philippine languages, which they cannot understand, go away saying, 'it is just like Rome.' Except for the colorful liturgical procedure, the contrary is true. . . . The visitors see only the setting of the Church and hear the stately liturgy. They leave without knowing the teaching." (1942, 98–9)

There are then several teaching points on which members of the UUCP can focus, areas of profound ignorance in their western brothers' and sisters' education. First, as self-evident as this may seem, the Philippines is an Asian, third-world nation. Prior to now, this has not been a context in which Unitarian Universalism emerges and flourishes: the economic disparities and cultural dissimilarities are extreme and often hard to understand. The UUCP is Unitarian Universalism in a context unlike anything most could conceive. Learning and understanding as much as one can about the Philippines and life on Negros must be a priority to any further or new relationships with these congregations. This will be an important first step.

Second, we will have to recognize that there are essential theological differences between the UUCP and most western Unitarian Universalists: the UUCP is thoroughly Christian (and some are trinitarians). Many Philippine Unitarian Universalists are exasperated that

western Unitarian Universalists don't seem to understand, appreciate, and accept their theological stance, because they see themselves as following in the traditions
of Murray Universalism and Aglipayan Unitarianism,
heritages that are documented and held in esteem.
Becoming more familiar with Christian Unitarian
Universalism (pre- and postmerger), domestically and
internationally, is paramount to a balanced relationship
with the UUCP.

Finally, while there are obvious and glaring differences in our contexts, and though our theology may sound
quite different, we share principles that have character-
ized Unitarian Universalism worldwide: the principles of
freedom, reason, and tolerance. It's these principles that
attract our Filipino brothers and sisters to liberal religion.
They don't share the commonly held characteristics of
North Atlantic Unitarian Universalism: they are not economically secure, but are a church of the poor; they are not
well educated, by our standards some would consider
them illiterate; they are just beginning to introduce professional ministry to their movement, but for now most of
the UUCP ministers are peasant farmers. But like western Unitarian Universalists, they have a deep and profound desire to know truth and meaning, and they don't
believe that there is a single way for finding it. They have
a thirst to know and do what is right. To this desire and
quest they bring their historical and cultural traditions as
well as their social, economic, and political realities. These
conditions might lead many westerners to cower and turn
away from our religious quests. But for Filipinos, the
depth and richness of their emerging Unitarian Universalist tradition is broad and eclectic, and holds promise.

We have much to learn from those who have not
grown accustomed to the material and programs of our
western way of congregational life—buildings, adminis-
trators, a professional ministry, organized religious education. The UUCP doesn't assume any of this. Yet they
embrace the liberal faith with enthusiasm, for what it is
and means—the free and responsible search for truth and

meaning. What they hold up as important and meaning-
ful may feel or sound orthodox to us, but given their context and history, for them their faith is heretical—it is
their chosen faith.

So much of what I have seen, heard, and experienced
is captured in correspondence with the Rev. Pere Carl
Quimada Sienes, a 1995 graduate of Silliman University
Divinity School who now serves in the Philippine Navy
and is living in Manila. Early in my visit I had given Pere
Carl a copy of *With Purpose and Principle.* After he read
the book, he wrote a letter that raises issues and concerns
he has, in a Philippine Unitarian Universalist context; his
letter also reflects thoughtfulness, sincerity, and commitment to the future leadership of the UUCP.

> Fred,
>
> May the things for Peace be done.
>
> For the past days, even years, I thought Unitarian
> Universalism is just all about freedom of thought and
> expression, and the on-going quest to understand better
> that "something somewhere" whom we pay deep
> reverence. But I realized it's more than that; that Liberal
> Christianity moved by ethics "seems" the same. I would
> say that Christianity is more than the belief of God and
> Jesus Christ but to be a true Christian is to live a life in
> accordance to Jesus' message: to feed the hungry, release
> the captives, love God by loving thy neighbor. . . . So Jesus
> was working for a community where justice, equity and
> compassion abounds. He intended to work for a "heaven
> on earth." And this is what our Principles and Purposes
> are referring to. Am I right?
>
> I'm reading a book about the challenges of diversity.
> My seminary thoughts on "fairness," which our 3rd
> principle talks about was reinforced by this book,
> especially Luke's views of social justice and John's views
> of eternal life (a life of peace in this world). I see it as a
> challenge for every human being who is focused on a
> better world, for a "heaven on earth." But it's so hard,
> almost impossible especially in our times today. How can
> fairness (our 3rd principle) be realized in a democratic

society where fairness means an equal share of life's
needs? Do you think I'm on the right track? Does the 4th
principle refer to that quest of "something somewhere"
whom reverence is paid and/or it also refers to the
continuous quest for the modern world's destiny? If so,
would not modernization be an obstacle to the realization
of the 3rd principle?
Please share your thoughts.

    With you on that quest,

    Pere Carl

I wrote back:

    Dear Pere,

    It was good to talk with you and for you to remind me
to respond to your letter. I will address the issues you raise.
    First, something about my essay in Edward Frost's
book. The book is about our "Principles and Purposes"—all
of them. My essay addresses only the 4th Principle [We
affirm and promote a free and responsible search for truth
and meaning]. When I wrote it, I knew there were several
things I had to be conscious of: that I would be writing for
a large, wide audience with a variety of beliefs. As it is,
there are probably those who don't like my essay simply
because I talked about God. Also, I felt constrained from
writing about social justice, fairness, ethics and democracy
since these all would be covered in other essays. In this
sense, the essays, as do the Principles, must be read as
supportive of each other and not independent of each
other. My essay is not necessarily about God, but about the
free and responsible search. But in order for the search to
make sense, something must be said about the search's
objective, which is—according to our Principles—truth and
meaning. Truth and meaning come in many shapes and
sizes, even for those using the same words—like God. But,
for our search to be free and responsible, this requires
honesty and above all, I tried to be honest in my essay just
as we all need to be honest in our searches.
    Being on a search does not rule out fairness, justice
and ethical behavior. In fact, many have argued that some

who say they know God, believe in Jesus and the Holy
Spirit (or Allah or you name the deity) and in this sense
are not on a search at all for they have found their
religion—some say that these people are the most
dangerous and some of these orthodox (which means right
belief) are the most unjust, unfair and undemocratic
people of all. What's my point? My point is that freedom of
thought, expression and searching are a big part of liberal
religion, certainly not all of it but again, the 4th Principle
is just one of seven. Unfortunately there are Unitarian
Universalists who are in it only for the search and that's
too bad because this is very one-dimensional and religion
is more than searching, more than faith (or the lack of it).
It's both faith and works, right?

Now, about Jesus' ministry in Luke and John. Of
course Jesus' message and life were about social justice
and fairness, and a lot more. Someone has noted that the
purpose of the church (or religion or Christianity, but let's
say the church) is to afflict the comfortable and comfort
the afflicted. It's both pastoral and prophetic, spirituality
and liberation. Any time you become just one or the other,
you're out of balance and one-dimensional. I've seen too
many ministers who preach and teach from just one
dimension and to do this is not being honest with your
congregation, with Unitarian Universalism or oneself.
This means a ministry to all people—the sick and healthy,
the poor and rich, the unfavored and favored.

This raises another issue, one about fairness. If you
believe in God—whatever or whomever that God is—does
your God "play favorites." I'm thinking about liberation
theologians who say that God has a preference for the
poor (the downtrodden, the despised). This was an issue
I tried to deal with in my book (*A Reason for Hope*). If
God does have a preference for the poor, then you and I
are serving the wrong people! Neither my congregation
in Annapolis or the Philippine Navy have much to do
with serving the outcasts and despised, those with
whom—some say—God sides. Or is there another way
to think about this? I think there is. And that's why I
wrote my book.

Finally, this—you ask about fairness in the world. I've
quit thinking about the world as the place for my mission.

Of course, I can't ever completely forget about the world,
but what I mean is that too many people end up going
nowhere with their agenda and good intentions because
they've set such gigantic goals (like world peace, justice
for all people) that they will never achieve their goals.
Goals need to be specific, attainable and measurable—
something within grasp, preferably in one's lifetime.
Which is why I love work in the church (and I know you
do too). In the context of my church (and Unitarian
Universalism), I can help to make real change—I can
work for it, see it, feel it. In our church we create just
relations, we care for each other in a loving way, we
respect people no matter what—I see and feel it, and
others do too: that's why the church has been growing.
And in living the Principles, we model (set examples) for
our children and for the greater community. We are saying
"See, it can work; it can be done; we can live and work
together in a fair and equitable way." Of course, it doesn't
always work, but 450 members is a lot easier to work with
than several billion. At least it's a place to start. Does this
mean I don't work in the larger community? Of course
not, I do what I can there too. But my primary efforts are
serving my congregation and the greater UU church,
doing what I can to change the world through these
smaller arenas. That is in part what I think the ministry
and the church is all about—that's both faith and works.
If you can read between the lines, this is why you must
return to the church, to the local church. If you want to
make changes in people's lives, in their worlds, then it's
going to happen in the church. By the way, at the
beginning of our Principles, it states: "We covenant to
affirm and promote. . . . " Covenant is the commitment we
make to each other in religious community—not as
isolated individuals, but in community. We enter the
covenant as individuals but in covenant we agree to be
and work together. In other words, the Principles are to be
lived out and worked for in church, with church.

   About modernization—fundamentalists in all religions
fear modernity. I have no problem with the modern life
(I'm writing this letter to you on a laptop computer!). It all
depends on how modernization is used—to balance or
create an imbalance between people? There's very little we

can do about modernization—it's a fact of life. There's a phrase that's been used in the States: if we're going to have high tech, then we need high touch. Which is to say: when modernization is used in such a way that isolates people, takes them out of community and relation, and pits people against people, then modernization is hurtful. If modernization can empower people, bring them together and serve us, then this is good.

So, I've rambled on enough. I look forward to the day when I hear that you have returned to Negros, are playing soccer with Lupe Karl, spending Sunday evenings with Lundy Mae and serving a congregation, justice and your God.

Best wishes and take care,

Fred

I'm shocked to hear some suggest that the Unitarian Universalist congregations emerging and developing in the Philippines and in other emerging-nation contexts can't really be Unitarian Universalist—and I know that leaders like Pere Carl would be shocked too. Given the three historical branches of our movement, Eastern European, British, and North American; given what I've observed at any Unitarian Univeralist general assembly, where you can find everything from Pagans to Buddhists to Christians to Jews (all under the banner of Unitarian Universalism), I don't understand what some mean when they suggest our Philippine brothers and sisters aren't really Unitarian Universalists.

Let us embrace the affirmation and growth of the liberal faith in emerging-nation contexts as an unprecedented challenge. It's about the challenge of colonialism: an attitude that promoted western imperialism, an attitude that oozed into every area of life in most postcolonial contexts. It's about classism: the separation of people by false dichotomies created by materialism. There's challenge of ethnocentrism: a worldview that elevates our way of living and believing as the best way. It's about the paradigm of values that we have taken for granted as intrinsic to the Unitarian Universalist faith: outside our western context, the North Atlantic perspective may not fit. The UUCP, like others in emerging-nation Unitarian Universalist settings, is challenging the very essence of our liberal faith. May we too be Maglipay Universalists, "joyful Universalists," embracing them in love and in the spirit of the religious heritage we share.

Questions for Discussion

1. "The UUCP . . . is a rural peasant church. . . . Remaining a church of the poor will not [however] sustain a robust future for the church—it won't satisfy the emerging leadership." As the North Atlantic UU community strengthens its relationship with the UUCP, how might our very different demographics and theologies challenge and inspire us?

2. "There are important lessons for us to learn from the past fifty years." Discuss these lessons.

3. In the letter from Pere Carl Quimada Sienes, he writes: "Jesus was working for a community where justice, equity and compassion abounds. He intended to work for a 'heaven on earth.' And this is what our Principles and Purposes are referring to. Am I right?" How would you respond?

Children of the UU congregation in Caican, Santa Catalina, Negros Oriental.

Children singing at the congregation in Malingin, Bago City, Negros Occidental.

Rev. Rebecca Sienes, right, and two members of the Banaybanay congregation stand on the future site of the church.

Susan Quisel, a divinity school student, performs her practicum—a child dedication.

Appendix 1

Unitarians Face a New Age
The Commission of Appraisal of the
American Unitarian Association, 1936
Excerpt from Chapter IX
"International Relations of the American
Unitarian Association"
by
Louis C. Cornish

Independent Church of the Philippines

When he was Secretary of the Department of Foreign Relations, the late Rev. Charles W. Wendte learned of the great trek from the Roman Church in the Philippines. Millions of people deserted the Catholic faith under the leadership of several men, among whom the chief was Gregorio Aglipay, formerly a Roman Catholic priest who had been doing the work of a bishop. Dr. Wendte began correspondence with Archbishop Aglipay. William Howard Taft became Governor of the Islands and extended advice and friendliness to the Independent Church. He later became its Honorary President.

In 1928 Major Connor arrived in Cambridge. He had been for seventeen years Judge Advocate in the Philippines. A unitarian himself, a friend of Archbishop Aglipay, he recommended a more active fellowship. The Twenty-Fifth Anniversary of the Independent Church was approaching. We sent two commissioners to present greetings, Rev. Eugene R. Shippen, D.D., and Rev. Berkeley B. Blake, D.D. For a number of weeks they made a thorough investigation of the Independent Church and reported that it was an earnest movement of great worth.

They recommended later that we bring the Archbishop and a traveling companion to this country. Other American Unitarians visited the church and testified favorably. Devoted Unitarians in this country made possible a visit of the Archbishop and his companion, Bishop de los Reyes, the Metropolitan of Manilla, to this country. They spoke in a number of our churches and were eagerly welcomed. The Meadville School conferred the degree of D.D. upon the Archbishop. President Hoover received them at Washington. They were welcomed by the denomination at the Annual Meeting in Boston. They again visited us, and at their own expense, in the spring of 1934 on their way to the International Congress in Copenhagen.

The Philippine Church has a membership of about 4,000,000 people. We have given no money, nor have we ever been asked to do so, but we have given counsel and we are assured that our friendship has given great encouragement to a church which is in constant conflict with the Roman Catholic Church and which desires to stand in active fellowship with all liberal churches in the world.

The President has just received the following letter from Archbishop Aglipay, quoted in part,

"Taking advantage of the first trans-Pacific flight of the 'Philippine Clipper,' I write you this fraternal message to convey to you and the Churches of the Unitarian Fellowship my Christmas greetings and best wishes for a happy new year. I also extend my greetings to all of our liberal friends on that continent."

Appendix 2

The Biography of Rev. Toribio S. Quimada
by
Melca Quimada Legaje*

On April 27, 1917 a healthy baby boy, Toribio S. Quimada, came into this beautiful world from poor parents, Mr. Zoilo Quimada and Juliana Sabandija. His father's job was carpentry and he went to nearby towns and cities to do carpentry jobs so to feed his big family. Zoilo also went to the farms to augment his livelihood. Toribio was one of thirteen children: seven boys and six girls. He was second to the eldest. During these times Filipino families were usually big families (especially those living in the mountains) because family planning techniques were not introduced at that time. Toribio went to Minglanilla Elementary School for his elementary education from 1927–1933 in Minglanilla, Cebu City. He really was very interested to continue his studies in the high school but because of family pressures he helped his brothers and sisters manage their farms while his father was out of the house at work.

During evenings or leisure times, Toribio, especially in his younger years, often heard his parents discuss religion and he always heard his father criticize the Protestant church and its principles (because the Quimadas were active Catholics at the time). In their discussions, they also criticized the Bible having heard that it was made by Martin Luther: Luther buried it inside a big live tree and that after many years, by a dream, such tree was found and opened and there the Bible was found. So the neighbors with his parents despised the Bible. Toribio

* Melca is the granddaughter of Toribio Quimada and the wife of the Rev. Henry Legaje.

wanted to see and read the Bible, but the Roman Catholics forbid reading the book.

In 1935, the Great Depression came to Cebu Province which made residents vacate or move to other places to look for a better living. Zoilo and his family went to Nataban, San Carlos City, Negros Occidental to establish another livelihood in October 1936. Toribio was newly married this year to Sergia Talandron. Fernando Quimada [Zoilo's brother], of Nataban, a Protestant leader in that area, helped them with their move despite the hurtful words from Zoilo about Protestant families in Nataban. They lived and mingled with the Protestant families in Nataban. It was during this time that Toribio finally saw, read and owned a bible from Fernando. Toribio cherished this book for he learned wisdom from it.

Though a member of the Catholic Church, soon he started to attend Sunday worship at the Protestant church led by Fernando Quimada. He participated in their discussions even though he couldn't accept their way of teaching and their principles—he questioned them until he was satisfied. The church leaders often misunderstood him—they thought he was a critic and not a good Christian. But he continued attending Sunday Service even though they showed less interest in him.

During the Second World War, there were blackouts where people were not allowed to use kerosene lamps or any kind of lamps where the light could easily be seen or detected by Japanese fighter planes. During this time, Toribio's younger sister, Teopista, died. Toribio asked the Protestant church leader to perform the funeral. The Catholic leaders and members were shocked and wondered why Toribio did this. Starting with his sister's death, Toribio relied on the Protestant Church, not the Catholic Church, for services.

Toribio and his wife had ten children: Agapito, Santiago, Elizabeth, Felomine, Librada, Rebecca, Alexander, Deborah, Lydianita and a baby boy who died soon after birth. Still living are Agapito, Santiago, Librada, Rebecca, Deborah and Lydianita.

While actively involved with Protestant church activities, Toribio was made a teacher in the Sunday School and was often asked to give sermons on Sunday. His own parents, brothers and sisters and most especially the Catholic leaders and members were angry for spending so much time with the Protestants. There were even times or situations where Toribio's father would debate with him about Protestant principles.

In July 1943 during the height of WW II, Rev. Toribio Quimada's family accepted baptism which took place in his father's house. There were about two dozen (including his father) who became members of the *Iglesia Universal de Kristo*. In 1948, after the War, Toribio's minister, Francisco Hili became ill with anemia and could not serve anymore. The church's officers petitioned the General Minister of the *Iglesia Universal de Kristo* requesting that Toribio be ordained and to take the place of Rev. Hili. The request was granted and Toribio was ordained as a minister of the *Iglesia Universal de Kristo* on January 22, 1948, during the dedication of the newly organized church in Navididan, Prosperidad, San Carlos City. He was given the authority to solemnize marriages by Mr. Lucian Mercado that year.

The people involved in Toribio's ordination were Julian Baladjay, Donato Capilitan, Saturnino Rogero, Fortunato Arroyo, Esteban Apatan, Rev. Francisco Hili and Rev. Fernando Quimada. The event was a memorable one. The responsibilities that Toribio would face would be many, made more difficult by his lack of a high school education.

Additional congregations were created for Toribio to serve: Tayabana, Bnga and Napaturan all in San Carlos City, Negros Occidental, and in Negros Oriental additional congregations included Naliwangan, Pamplona and Tanja. There was some progress during his ministry and each member was supposed to have their own personal copy of a hymnbook, the Bible and Sunday School materials. When he was asked to be the Sunday School teacher this was the problem: no materials. The headquarters wouldn't provide these materials, so Toribio tried everything possible by making contacts with different Christian Philippine denominations as well as groups abroad. In 1951 he came across an article listing all the Christian churches organized in America. He looked for the letter "U" hoping to find Iglesia Universal de Kristo but he couldn't find it. Instead he found the Universalist Church of Wisconsin. This was the first time he had seen the word Universalist and he wondered what relationship it had to his church. Around this same time, a friend of his, Florencio Cabalquinto, had a World Almanac and in it was a list of churches in the U.S. He found the Universalist Church of Gloucester, Massachusetts. He wrote to the church in Wisconsin, but his letter was returned. So he wrote the church in Gloucester and the letter was received by Rev. Carol Westman and Toribio received a response on March 28, 1952, telling him how surprised he was to know about the Universalist Church in the Philippines. Westman also said that Toribio's letter had been forwarded to Rev. Carlton M. Fisher, Executive Director of the Universalist Service Committee. From then on Toribio continued his communication with the USC. Eventually, Toribio received books for his church and this made him very happy. He also received the "How To Know Your Bible" series which was helpful in his quest to know the Bible. These things led to his church superiors' anger at Toribio. They decided to excommunicate him from the church for the simple reason of his connections and his communications the Universalist Church of Gloucester in the U.S. In 1954, Toribio was expelled/excommunicated from *Iglesia Universal de Kristo* and his license to solemnize marriages was taken away. Another reason he was expelled was for not giving the 30% of his income to the church headquarters.

After Toribio was excommunicated, those members who sympathized with his plight joined him in his link to the Universalist Church of America. Letters of recommendation followed from the members of the city government such as Mayor, Vice-Mayor, Secretary, Judge, City

Health Doctor, Chief of Police, members of the city Council, Deputy Governor, and his followers from the *Iglesia
Universal de Kristo.*

On December 29, 1954, their request was granted by
the Universalist Church and from then on they were
counted as one of the Universalist congregations. The Universalist Church of the Philippines was finally recognized
by the Philippine government on April 25, 1955 after it
was registered with the Securities and Exchange Commission. On January 8, 1985, the UCP name was changed
to Unitarian Universalist Church of the Philippines.

In August 1958, a Japanese Universalist minister visited Toribio in Nataban. He was the first Universalist
foreigner/minister to observe Toribio's leadership. The
Japanese minister was Rev. Toshio Yoshioka. Rev. Yoshioka did a lot of teaching about Universalism in different
congregations, he made many home/church visits and he
stayed with Toribio for seven days. After his visit, he made
a report to Dr. Dana E. Klotzle. This year Toribio was also
sent to school by the UCP following Rev. Yoshioka's visit.
He was sent to Silliman University as a special student,
taking up the Bachelor of Theology program. There was a
condition made between him and the school that if he
could maintain the required grade point average then Silliman would ask the Bureau of Private Schools to give
him a special examination so that he could be considered
a regular college student. He was considered a special student because he had no high school education. Sadly he
did not make it. He did not pass the school requirement
regarding GPA so he studied at Calatrava Public High
School for his last two years of high school education. He
graduated from the high school and moved his family to
Dumaguete City where he went to Foundation University
where he studied elementary education. He entered the
University in 1960 and received his degree in 1965. All
the expenses incurred from his studies as well as his family expenses were borne by the UUA. While in Dumaguete, he was asked by Dr. Klotzle to go to Manila and
meet an American visitor. On August 23, 1964, he took his

first plane ride to meet Rev. Richard Boeke at the Manila YMCA. The following day, a meeting was held with Toribio, Boeke and Bishop Angel Bitanga. Toribio would make a second trip, later, to Manila for the arrival of Dr. Dana Maclean Greely, Dr. Charles Vickery and Dr. Max Gaebler. Another American Universalist minister visited Dumaguete in 1965. This was Rev. Robert Swain. From Dumaguete, Toribio brought Swain to Nataban, San Carlos City where the annual convention was held. Rev. Swain took the plane from Bacolod to Manila.

After Toribio finished his college education, he and his family decided not to go back to Nataban but instead looked for farmland to purchase. The reason for this move was because Nataban was so far away from everything: it took five to six hours to walk on foot to leave the mountains. There was no means of transportation other than horseback. At that time, the Universalist Church of the Philippines acquired church materials and equipment such as a typewriter, mimeographing machines, books, filing cabinets, etc., which couldn't be moved to Nataban because of the difficult conditions. Therefore, land in Nagbinlod was bought along a private road. This was also the home of the UCP national headquarters.

The UCP was accepted into membership by the International Association for Religious Freedom in 1972. In January 1985, "Unitarian" was registered with the Philippine Securities and Exchange Commission. Then Toribio began working on application for membership to the UUA. February 1988 saw two visitors come to Cawitan as a result of Toribio's request for UUA membership. The first to arrive was Rev. Richard Boeke, followed by Rev. Melvin Hoover. Later, Lucie Meijer and Frauke Smidth of the IARF visited. The group was joined by an American UU Peace Corps Volunteer, Jorie Agate, who taught Sign Language at Silliman University.

On May 23, 1988, Toribio met his horrible death. He was shot to death and was burned, with all church materials and equipment. He was scheduled to travel to the UUA General Assembly with Rev. Perfecto Sienes for the probable acceptance of the UUCP's application for membership into the UUA. Even his horse was shot to death. He had been using this horse on his travels to the mountains, conducting marriages and baptisms and other church-related activities. On June 19, 1988, the UUCP application for UUA membership was finally accepted. Happy but sad were the ringing words of the two UUCP delegates to the UUA General Assembly—Rev. Perfecto Sienes and Mrs. Rebecca Quimada Sienes—during their short speeches at the Assembly in response to the acceptance which should have been made by the Rev. Toribio S. Quimada.

This is the life of the late Rev. Toribio Sabandija Quimada, the founder of the Unitarian Universalist Church of the Philippines.

Appendix 3

The Constitution and Bylaws

Unitarian Universalist Church of the Philippines
065 Rovira Road, Bantayan, Dumaguete City
Negros Oriental, Philippines 6200

Approved and Amended
April 1999 Annual Convention

UNITARIAN UNIVERSALIST CHURCH OF THE PHILIPPINES, INC.

CONSTITUTION & BYLAWS

UUCP Mission Statement

We believe in a loving God and a just, helpful and caring community. We affirm to promote the welfare of the environment and support for a just and economic, social and spiritual connection that will lead to build an open mind for a wholistic life. We affirm to uphold an equal and peaceful relationship to every person and to every religion because we are here as One Big Family.

ARTICLE I
NAME

The name of this Church shall be the UNITARIAN UNIVERSALIST CHURCH OF THE PHILIPPINES, INC.

ARTICLE II
NATIONAL OFFICE

The National Office of the Church shall be at 065 Rovira Road, Bantayan, 6200 Dumaguete City, Negros Oriental, Philippines.

ARTICLE III
PRINCIPLES & PURPOSES

Section 1. Principles

We, the members of the Unitarian Universalist Church of the Philippines, Inc., covenant to affirm and promote:

1. There is only one God who is the God of Love;
2. The inherent worth and dignity of every person;
3. Human relation must be dealt with justice, equality, and compassion;

4. Accept and encourage each others spiritual growth;
5. The right to conscience and the use of democratic process in any undertaking;
6. A free and responsible search for truth and meaning;
7. To build a world community with peace, liberty, and justice for all;
8. The respect of the interdependent web of all existence of which we are a part.

These living traditions which we share draws from many sources:

1. Direct experience of that Transcending Power of mystery and wonder, affirmed in all cultures, which moves us to a renewal of the spirit and openness to the forces, which create and uphold life;
2. Words and deeds of prophetic men and women which challenge us to powers and structures of evil justice, compassion and transforming it through the power of love;
3. Wisdom from the world's religions which inspires us in our ethical and spiritual life;
4. Jewish and Christian teachings which calls us to respond to God's love by loving our neighbors as ourselves;
5. Humanist teachings, which counsel us to heed the guidance of reason and the results of science and warn us against of the mind and spirit.

Section 2. Purposes

The Unitarian Universalist Church of the Philippines, Inc., shall devote its resources and exercise its corporate powers for religious, educational and humanitarian purposes. The Church shall help its members uplift their economic lives; strengthen their relationships with one another and to the One whom they pay deep homage. It shall encourage the members to express freely their beliefs, opinions, and views, to use the democratic process in every undertaking, and to work for a better world to live with peace, liberty, and justice for all with respect of all existence of which we are a part.

ARTICLE IV
THE CHURCH MEMBERSHIP

Section 1. Individual Membership

Any person can be a member to a congregation or fellowship provided that such applicant shall subscribe to the Principles and Purposes; shall have adequate knowledge about Unitarianism and Universalism; and pledges to support the ministry of the Church.

Section 2. Group Membership

An organized group can become a member of the Unitarian Universalist Church of the Philippines provided that the applicant has at least twenty five (25) members; shall subscribe to the Principles and purposes; shall have necessary knowledge about Unitarianism and Universalism; and pledges to support the ministry of the Church.

Paragraph 1. Procedures

An organized group may become a member congregation or fellowship by submitting a written application to the Extension Department of the Unitarian Universalist Church of the Philippines for evaluation. After its thorough evaluation, the Chairperson of the Extension Department recommends it to the Board of Directors who shall scrutinize and discuss further its intention before giving it to the Convention for final approval.

Paragraph 2. Composition of the Letter

The application letter shall consist of the following:

1. A written statement that the applicant subscribes to the Principles and Purposes;
2. A written statement that the applicant pledges to support the Church,
3. The letter shall state the reasons for its interest of joining;

4. It must be signed by all its officers and majority of its members;

5. It shall also include the list of all the members and other necessary information(s) needed to support the application such as its history.

The group must send representative(s) to the Annual Convention of the Unitarian Universalist Church of the Philippines to witness the deliberation of their application and to answer question(s) about its intention from the delegates of the Convention.

ARTICLE V
THE OFFICERS OF THE CHURCH

Section 1. Elected Officers

The elected officers of the Unitarian Universalist Church of the Philippines, Inc., shall be the Moderator, President, Vice President, Secretary, Treasurer, and Auditor. An elected officer shall be elected in a Convention declared Quorum and shall take office after being installed before the Convention ends.

Paragraph 1. The Moderator

The Moderator presides all plenary sessions of every Convention of the Church. He/She shall present the Church on special occasions and shall assist in promoting its welfare.

Paragraph 2. The President

The President shall be the Chief Executive of the Church; a member of all standing departments, organizations, and the BOD without a vote. In case of a tie, the President breaks the tie. He/She shall be authorized to act, execute, implement, report, sign, represent, and monitor the approved programs and make recommendations for and in behalf of the Church. However, if the case is not emergency in nature, such action shall wait for the approval by the Board.

Paragraph 3. The Vice President

The Vice President shall have such powers and perform such duties as may be assigned by the Board or the President and shall be a member of the BOD.

Paragraph 4. The Secretary

The Secretary shall be a member of the Board. He/She prepares the Minutes of the following meetings. Executive Committee Meetings, Board of Director's Meetings, Annual Convention. The respective Chairperson(s) shall sign the Minutes of the EXECOM & BOD, while, the Moderator, for authentication purposes shall sign the Minutes of the Annual Convention.

The Secretary keeps all the records, supervises elections, and represents the Church to special occasions and assists in promoting the welfare of the Church.

Paragraph 5. The Treasurer

The Treasurer withdraws and disburses funds of the approved programs and a bank signatory. He/She renders financial report every regular Board Meeting and Annual Convention. The church funds and properties as well as the corporate seal shall be under the care and custody of the treasurer. The treasurer advises the President and the Board about the over-all finances of the Church. Furthermore, she/he shall be a BOD member.

A. Financial Secretary

The Financial Secretary is an appointed position of the Church classified not as an officer who shall assist the treasurer of looking into the overall finances of the Church. He/She shall be responsible in preparing the financial statement for the basis of treasurer's report, in charge of all bookkeeping transaction.

B. *Resignation of a Financial Secretary*

The Financial Secretary may resign anytime by giving a written notice to the Board or to the President. Such resignation shall take effect only after all records, in his/her custody, are cleared by the Treasurer and the Auditor.

C. *Relinquished Records from the Financial Secretary*

All records that has been under the custody of the Financial Secretary shall be handed over to the Secretary of the Church for safe keeping purposes before a newly appointed Financial Secretary is available and set to office.

D. *Removal of a Financial Secretary*

A financial secretary may be removed upon the written recommendation by the Treasurer concerned or by the Auditor addressed to the BOD or to the President. The letter shall state the reason(s) for removal. Such removal shall take place only after all records under his/her custody are cleared by the Treasurer and the Auditor.

Paragraph 6. The Auditor

The auditor audits all funds, acquired properties, and gives his/her report every Annual Convention.

Section 2. Term of Office

Paragraph 1. An Elected Officer

An elected officer shall serve for a term of four (4) years and until his/her successor is elected and installed. No elected officer shall serve for more than two consecutive terms. Any partial term of more than two (2) years served by reason of appointment shall be considered a full term.

Paragraph 2. An Appointed Officer

An appointed officer shall serve for the remaining un-exposed term of the officer he/she is replacing with. The Board shall have the power to appoint or will be responsible of looking for a replacement.

Section 3. Qualification of an Officer

An officer shall be a resident of the Philippines; a member of a certified congregation or fellowship of the Church; and shall have the time to serve such office to the best of his/her knowledge and ability. If such officer does not qualify to the stated provisions, he/she shall be disqualified and the office shall be declared vacant.

Section 4. Election & Appointment of an Officer

All officers shall be elected during an Annual Convention that is declared Quorum. Appointments shall be done during the Board Meeting that is declared quorum. However, if the case calls for an immediate action, the Executive Committee and/or the President may act, provided that such action is for the best interest and welfare of the Church.

Section 5. Removal of an Officer

Paragraph 1. An Elected Officer

An elected officer except the Treasurer may be removed by a three-fourths (3/4) vote of the entire Board at a meeting of which not less than three-fourths of the entire Board is present. If in the opinion of the Board such officer is incapacitated or unable to carry out the duties of such office or has been found guilty of immoral, unethical or improper conduct as mandated in Article XII of the Bylaws. The President may also be removed by such a vote by the Board, if it determines that such removal is in the best interest of the Church. In the case of the Treasurer, he/she can be removed only after having been cleared by the Auditor.

Paragraph 2. An Appointed Officer

Any appointed officer may be removed from office at any time by the Board in a meeting declared quorum. However if the case calls for an immediate action, the Executive Committee may act provided that such action is for the best interest and welfare of the Church.

Section 6. Resignation of an Officer

An Officer except the treasurer may resign at anytime by giving a written notice to the Board or to the President. Such resignation shall take effect at the time specified therein, or if no time is specified, then upon delivery. For the case of the treasurer, she/he has to be cleared by the Auditor.

Section 7. Vacancies

Paragraph 1. Elected Officer

A vacancy created by death, disqualification, resignation or removal of an elected officer may filled by the Board until which an election can be held. The vacancy shall be then be filled by election for the remaining unused term, if any.

Paragraph 2. Appointed Officer

A vacancy created by death, disqualification, resignation, or the Board may fill removal of any appointed officer for the balance of the unused term.

Section 8. Reports by Officers

The President, the Treasurer, and the Auditor will make a report every Board Meeting and every Church Convention.

Section 9. Compensation

An elected or appointed officer may receive compensation for their services provided that there are funds available for compensation. Such decision must be subject to the approval of the Annual Convention.

Section 10. The Executive Committee

The Executive Committee shall consist of the President, the Vice President, the Secretary, and the Treasurer. The Committee shall conduct the ordinary and current business of the Church; supervises, appoints, implements, and evaluates approved programs between meetings of the Board. In between meetings of the Board, when issues or matters arise which in the opinion of the Committee are not current and ordinary business, and need immediate attention, in the best interest of the Church must be acted thereon for the Board. But only if three (3) of the four (4) members vote the action.

Paragraph 1. Presiding Officer

The President may be its Presiding Officer or can appoint one member of the Committee.

Paragraph 2. Time and Place of Meetings

The Committee shall hold the meeting at such a time and place as it may determine.

Paragraph 3. Call and Notice of Meetings

Meetings of the Committee shall be initiated by the President at the request of, at least two (2) of his/her members. Notice for such meeting may be given in such manner and within such time, as the committee shall determine.

ARTICLE VI
THE BOARD OF DIRECTORS

Section 1. Responsibility

The Board shall conduct the affairs of the Church and subject to the Bylaws shall carry out the Church's policies and directives as provided by law.

Section 2. Powers

The Board shall act, appoint, supervise, and monitor for the Church in-between church conventions. All approved policies and programs during the Board meeting are subject to the approval of the Annual Convention. However, if the case calls for immediate action, the Board acts on behalf of the Assembly, but such action must be for the best interest of the Church. All existing programs of the Church shall be under the Board's supervision and evaluation.

Section 3. Membership

The Board of Directors shall consist of the following:

A. President, Vice President, Secretary, Treasurer, and Auditor
B. Chairpersons of every Department
C. Presidents of every Organization, and
D. Director elected at-large

Section 4. Term of Office

Paragraph 1. Automatic Director

A director governed by Section 3 (A & B) of this Article, shall have a term of office set in Article V Section 2; Article VII Section 4 of this bylaws, while Directors governed by Section 3 (C) of this Article, shall have a term in accordance to the organization's bylaws.

Paragraph 2. Director Elected-At-Large

The director elected-at-large shall take office after he/she has been installed during the Annual Convention. He/she shall serve for a term of four (4) years until his/her successor has been elected or appointed and installed. No director elected at large shall serve more than two (2) consecutive full terms of four (4) years each.

Section 5. Election of Directors

Directors governed by Section 3 (A & B) of this Article, shall be elected by the conditions set in Article V Section 4, & Article VII Section 4 respectively. The director-at-large shall be elected during the Annual Convention. The Directors governed by Section 3 (C) of this Article shall be elected by the condition set in accordance to the organization's bylaws.

Section 6. Qualification for Directorship

Directors governed by Section 3 (A & B) of this Article, shall be qualified on the basis set in Article V Section 3, and Article VII Section 5, of this bylaws, while the director governed by Section 3 (D) of Article VI shall be qualified on the basis of Article V Section 3 of this bylaws. The Directors governed by Section 3 (C) of this Article shall be qualified in accordance to the provision stated in their organizational bylaws.

Section 7. Resignation of the Board Member

Directors governed by Section 3 (A, B, C, & D) of this Article except the Treasurer shall resign in accordance to Article V Section 6 and Article VII Section 7 of this bylaws.

Section 8. Removal of a Board Member

The Directors governed by section (A, B, & D) of this Article except the Treasurer, shall be removed in accordance to Article V Section 5 and or Article VII Section 5 of this bylaws. While the Directors governed by Section 3 (c) of this Article, shall be removed in accordance to the policies raised in this Section and or in accordance to the provisions stated in the organization's bylaws.

Section 9. The Chairperson of the Board

The President of the Church and or the Board shall have the sole authority to designate the Chairperson from one of its members by appointment. In the best opinion, the Board shall have the authority to remove the Chairperson anytime. Such action may be mandated through incapacity to carry out the duties of chairmanship or found guilty of immoral, unethical or improper conduct as mandated in Article XII of this bylaws. Such decision must constitute a 3/4 consensus of the entire BOD of which the 3/4 numbers of the Board are present in a meeting.

Paragraph 1. Powers

The Chairperson of the Board shall preside the meeting and discussion of its agenda(s). He/she shall only vote to break a decision.

Paragraph 2. Term of Chairmanship

A Chairperson shall serve for one (1) whole fiscal year of the church or by a term determined by the Board.

Section 10. Vacancies

A vacancy created due to death, disqualification, resignation or removal from the office of the Board and such is governed by Section 3 (A, B, & D) of Article VI, shall be filled in accordance to Article V Section 7 and Section 4 of Article V of this bylaws. While vacancy created with the same causes as stated above and such is governed by Section 3 (C) of this Article, shall be filled in accordance to the provisions stated in the organization's bylaws.

Section 11. Place of Meeting

The Board shall hold its meeting at such places as the members may determine.

Section 12. Regular Meetings

Regular meetings of the Board shall be held at such time as the members shall determine, but not less than two (2) regular meetings shall be held during the whole year.

Section 13. Special Meetings

Special meetings of the Board may be initiated by the President of the Church at the request of, at least four (4) directors. Notice of special meetings shall be given in such time and manner as the Board shall determine, before the meeting and shall state the time and place of the meeting.

Section 14. Quorum

The majority of the entire Board shall constitute a Quorum.

Section 15. Compensation

Only the Director elected-at-large may receive an honorarium for his/her services provided funds are available for honorarium subject to the approval of the Annual Church Convention. All Directors maybe reimbursed as determine by the Board, subject to the approval of the Annual Convention for the expenses reasonably incurred by them in the performance of their duties.

Section 16. Annual Report

The Secretary shall, on behalf of the Board present or read the Minutes of its meeting to the Annual Convention and the previous Minutes of the Annual Convention.

ARTICLE VII
THE DEPARTMENTS OF THE CHURCH

Section 1. Standing Departments

The standing departments of the Church shall be the following:

- Religious Education Department
- Extension Department
- Finance & Planning Department

Paragraph 1. Religious Education Department

The department shall be responsible in offering curricula, resources, leadership training, religious education facilitators training; seek to be responsive and proactive religious developmental needs of the children, youths and adults.

A. Duties of the Chairperson and Its Staff(s)

The Chairperson and its Staff(s) shall make RE materials and facilitate in the implementation of approved programs, supervise, evaluate, and offer consultations on religious education concerns/issues at the local level.

Paragraph 2. Extension Department

The mission of the department shall focus on the development and strengthening of existing active congregation and fellowships committed to growth; inspire and reactivate inactive congregations and fellowships; and support changes that increase membership in the Unitarian Universalist Church of the Philippines, Inc.

A. Duties of the Chairperson and Its Staff(s)

The department members shall examine, explore, coordinate, and evaluate, and recommend new congregations and fellowships that wish to be recognized as member group of the church, to the Board, subject to the final evaluation of the Annual Convention.

Paragraph 3. Finance & Planning Department

The department shall work and plan for the yearly Church Convention and the future of the Church; make project proposals; assist the Extension Department in church growth and networks with other Unitarian Universalists and Ecumenical groups concerned with liberalism.

A. Duties of the Chairperson and Its Staff(s)

The members of the department shall be responsible in the following:

* preparing the agenda to be discussed during the Plenary Sessions of the Annual Convention
* arrange programs and meetings to be held in connection therewith
* certify and credentialize convention delegates, and
* plan ways to attain self-reliance.

Section 2. Appointment of Department Staff(s)

The department chairpersons shall have the authority to select its staff(s). The selection may be through appointment, however, appointee(s) are subject to Article VII Section 5 of this bylaws. However, if such staff does not qualify to the stated position he/she shall be disqualified and the position shall be declared vacant.

Section 3. Membership

Each department shall be headed by a Chairperson with two or three staff(s).

Section 4. Election and Term of Office

The Chairperson shall be elected by the Annual Convention. He/she shall serve for a term of four (4) years and until his/her successor is elected and installed. On the other hand, staff(s) shall only serve a term of three (3) years and until their successor is appointed and qualifies. No department member shall serve for more than two (2) consecutive terms.

Section 5. Qualification of a Chairperson/Staff

Each department Chairperson and staff shall be member of an accredited congregation or fellowship of the Church; a resident anywhere in the Philippines; and shall have time to serve the office to the best of his/her knowledge and ability.

Section 6. Removal of a Chairperson/Staff

Any Chairperson may be removed by a three-fourths (3/4) vote of the entire BOD at a meeting at which not less than three-fourths (3/4) of the entire BOD is present. If, in the opinion of the BOD such is incapacitated or otherwise unable to carry out the duties of the office or found guilty of immoral, unethical or improper conduct as mandated by Article XII of this bylaws. With the reasons stated, the Chairperson could remove any staff member from his/her office.

Section 7. Resignation of a Chairperson/Staff

Any chairperson may resign at any time by giving a written notice to the Board or the President of the Church. Such resignation shall take effect at the time specified therein, if no time is specified then upon delivery. A staff may resign by giving a written notice to the chairperson. The resignation shall take effect as stated above on the provisions of the department chairperson.

Section 8. Vacancies

A vacancy created by death, disqualification, resignation, or removal of an elected officer shall be filled by the Board until the next Convention of the Church, of which an election can be held. The vacancy shall be filled by the election for the balance of the unexposed term, if any. A vacancy of an appointed seat may be filled through an appointment.

Section 9. Additional Departments

Additional departments or sub-departments may be created or formed by the Board subject to the approval of the Annual Church Convention.

Section 10. Time and Place of Meetings

Each department shall hold its meetings at such time and place it may determine.

Section 11. Call and Notice of Meetings

Meetings of any department may be called by its chairperson and/or at the request of its members. Notice of this meeting shall be given in such manner and within such time as the members and the chair shall determine the agenda.

Section 12. Compensation

Any chairperson or staff(s) may receive an honorarium for their services, whenever there are funds available for compensation subject to the final approval of the Annual Convention.

Section 13. Quorum

The majority of the entire members of the Department shall constitute a quorum.

ARTICLE VIII
THE ORGANIZATION OF THE CHURCH

Section 1. Standing Organizations

The standing organizations of the Church shall be the following:

- Unitarian Universalist Ministers Association (UUMA)
- Unitarian Universalist Women Association (UUWA)
- Unitarian Universalist Youth Organization (UUYOP)
- Unitarian Universalist Faith Healers Association of the Philippines (UUFHP)
- Unitarian Universalist Men's Organization (UUMO)

Paragraph 1. Unitarian Universalist Ministers Association

The Association shall consist of all ordained ministers being fellowshipped by the Unitarian Universalist Church of the Philippines.

A. Duties of the President and Its Officers

The officers shall be responsible in administering the ministerial settlement process relating to all candidates for the ministry and the theological program, counsel the students, assist and organize the minister's training, represent the organization to special occasions, ordain, and install new candidates for the ministry, solve pastoral problems and conflicts, and recommend ordained minister for licensure, subject to the approval of the UUMA Assembly and its final approval by the Annual Church Convention.

Paragraph 2. Unitarian Universalist Women Association

The mission of this group is to unite the women and get acquainted for mutual support as well as personal and spiritual growth. This group works toward a future where women will be empowered to live their lives with the sense of wholeness and integrity in the world that recognizes the worth and dignity of every woman. It shall consist of all women of the Unitarian Universalist Church of the Philippines, Inc.

Paragraph 3. UU Youth Organization of the Philippines

The Unitarian Universalist Youth Organization enables the young UUs to join together for mutual support, personal growth, and spiritual enrichment in order to work for a better world where the youth are indeed real agents of change and hope of the church and society at large.

A. *Duties of the President and Its Officers*

They shall motivate, lead young people to think, make projects and create programs that the welfare of the youths and church, conduct conferences, retreats, and seminars, and organize the youth in the local levels.

Paragraph 4. Unitarian Universalist Faith Healers Association of the Philippines

The association shall enable and motivate its members to join together for mutual support, personal growth, and spiritual enrichment. They shall serve those who are in need, the sick, the bereaved, and those suffering from physical pain healing them to prayers to God, as a way of service to God, the greatest healer.

A. *Duties of the President and Its Officers*

They shall encourage its members to be open-minded, make project proposals that would benefit the group. The President shall preside all meetings of the group, sign on its behalf, and think for its best by planning for its future and to represent the group to special occasions.

Paragraph 5. Unitarian Universalist Men's Organization

This group enables the men of the Church to form into a group to help spread further the principles and purposes of Unitarianism Universalism. This group works toward personal growth and for mutual support to each other as well as spiritual enrichment in order to attain a better and a just society.

A. *Duties of the President and Its Officers*

The President shall preside in all meetings and shall lead in the planning of activities of the group. He shall encourage the men of the Church to join the group and actively participate in all its approved activities.

Section 2. Autonomy of Every Organization

Every organization of the Unitarian Universalist Church of the Philippines, Inc., shall have the autonomy and self-governed of its affair in planning and implementing programs, rules of conduct, policies, decide and elect its officers and to control its property and funds, but shall have direct supervision from the church officers and/or the Board.

The fiscal year budget of the standing organizations shall be subject to the approval of the Board of Directors and the Annual Convention.

Section 3. Membership

Each organization shall be headed by a President and the other official seats needed.

Section 4. Election and Term of Office

The President and its officers shall be elected by an assembly of the organization. They shall serve the term, described and written in its organizational bylaws, agree and approved by its assembly.

Section 5. Qualifications

The officers shall be qualified in accordance to the provision described and written in its organizational bylaws agreed and approved by its Assembly.

Section 6. Removal

An officer may be removed by a majority vote of its remaining officials in gathering, where majority of its members are present, if found to be incapacitated to carry out duties and responsibilities. An officer may be removed from office/position in accordance to provision(s) described and written in its organizational by-laws duly approved by its Assembly.

Section 7. Resignation

Any officer may resign at anytime by giving a written notice to its President, copy furnished to the UUCP President. In case where the President of the organization is the one who resigns then he/she shall give the written notice to his/her next in-lined officer, and copy furnished to the UUCP President. Any such resignation shall take effect at the time specified therein, or if no time specified, then upon delivery.

Section 8. Vacancies

A vacancy created by the death, disqualification, resignation or removal of an elected officer may be filled by the President of the Organization until the next assembly of such organization at which an election can be held. The vacancy shall be filled by election for the balance of the unexposed term, if any.

Section 9. Additional Organization

Additional organization may be created or formed by the Board provided such creation shall be approved by the Annual Church Convention.

Section 10. Time and Place of Meeting

Each organization shall hold the meetings at such time and place as it may be determined.

Section 11. Call and Notice of Meetings

The President at the request of its officers may initiate or call for a meeting. Such notice may be given in such manner and within such time, as the organization shall determine.

Section 12. Compensation

Any office of any organization may receive honorarium for their services, provided that funds are available for compensation, subject to the approval of its Assembly and the final approval shall be from the Annual Church Convention.

Section 13. Organizational Bylaws

Every organization of the UUCP shall formulate in writing its own bylaws. It shall include provisions for all policies, meetings and other information about the organizations' self-governance. A copy of these by-laws shall be given to the National Office for safekeeping and reference purposes, but such by-laws must be approved first by its Assembly.

ARTICLE IX
CHURCH CONVENTION

Section 1. The Convention

Each meeting of the Church for the conduct of business shall be called Convention.

Section 2. Powers and Duties

The Convention shall make overall policy for carrying out the purposes of the Church and shall direct and control its affairs.

Section 3. Regular Church Convention

A regular convention of the Unitarian Universalist Church of the Philippines, Inc., shall be held every April 22–27 of every year.

Section 4. Special Church Convention

A Special Church Convention may be called by the Board at any time, and shall be called upon written petition of not less than the majority of all accredited congregations and fellowships where such petition shall indicate the reason(s) for holding the Special Church Convention.

Section 5. Place of Meetings

Each Regular Church Convention shall be held at such place within the Philippine Archipelago, subject to the Convention's approval. However, Special Church Convention may be held at such place, as the Board shall determine.

Section 6. Notice of Meetings

Notice of each regular church convention shall be given not less than sixty (60) days before the date thereof in such form and manner as the Finance & Planning department with the Secretary may determine. Special Church Convention shall be given not less than three (3) weeks before the date. The notice shall state the place, date, and the hour of the meeting, which also include an indication at whose directive it is being called for, in the case of a Special Church Convention.

Section 7. Voting

Voting at each Church Convention Assembly shall be by certified delegates only. Each delegate shall only have one vote. Proxy voting is very much prohibited except for those "unable delegates" which means one who can't write or don't have arms to raise, if it's secret balloting or needs the raising of arms.

Section 8. Delegates

Each accredited congregation or fellowship shall be entitled to be represented at each Church Convention by as many delegates with each one being entitled to only one vote, if one a certified delegate.

Section 9. Certification of Delegates

Each participant from any accredited congregation or fellowship becomes a certified delegate after paying the registration fee of the amount that may be determined by the Board.

Section 10. Quorum

Majority of all certified delegates from the majority of all accredited congregation or fellowship shall constitute a quorum at any Church Convention.

ARTICLE X
THE MINISTRY OF THE CHURCH

Section 1. Autonomy of Congregations and Fellowships

Each accredited congregation or fellowship of the Unitarian Universalist Church of the Philippines, Inc., shall have the autonomy, self-governance of its own congregation or fellowship.

Paragraph 1. Congregational Polity

Nothing in this bylaws shall be construed as infringing upon the congregational polity or internal self-government of congregations or fellowships including the exclusive right of each congregations or fellowships to plan and implement programs, rules of conduct and policies, decide and elect its own officials and to control its property and funds.

Section 2. The Worship Formula

The Unitarian Universalist Church of the Philippines, Inc., shall have a worship formula. Such may be modified, so to fit a particular occasion but the essence of such guide should remain.

ORDER OF WORSHIP

Community Concern
Prelude
Lighting the Candle
Ringing the Bell
Call to Worship
Opening Hymn
Opening Prayer
Responsive Reading
Pastoral/Intercessory Prayer
Scripture/Poem Reading
Message through a song
Reflection/Sermon
Offertory
   Reading
   Song
   Offering
   Prayer of Thanks/Committal
Closing Hymn
Closing Prayer
Doxology
Benediction
Healing
Handshake for a Peace (with a song)

Section 3. The Ordained Religious Leaders

The ordained religious leaders of the Church shall be the Minister, the Elder, and the Deacon or Deaconess.

Paragraph 1. The Minister

He/she shall be responsible in nurturing its parishioners as to their role in the ministry, preach and teach Unitarianism and Universalism, its principles, the Bible, and other sacred religious writings than can be used as a guide for ethical living, serve the community by comforting those in sorrow and pain, visiting the sick and the prisoners, helping uplift the spirit of the oppress and the needy, conduct and perform worship services. He/she may represent his/her congregation or fellowship to special occasions and lead in promoting its welfare.

A. Compensation

Ordained Ministers settled in fellowships or congregations may be received compensation of an amount determined by the Board for their services, whether full-time or in tent-ministry, provided that funds are available for compensation, subject to the approval of the Annual Church Convention.

Paragraph 2. The Elder

He/she shall be responsible in assisting its minister in attending to the spiritual welfare and discipline of the church membership; help in implementing, supervising and evaluating church programs and policies of the congregation or fellowship especially the matters that affect the congregation or fellowship including the safeguard of church discipline, and do charitable works for the society of which he/she lives.

Paragraph 3. Deacon & Deaconess

Shall be responsible in formulating stewardship programs of the congregation or fellowship and oversees its implementation effectively. He/she shall do charitable works for the society of which he/she lives.

Section 4. The Ordination

Any member of the Unitarian Universalist Church of the Philippines, Inc., can be ordained as a religious leader provided that such applicant is an active member of any accredited congregation or fellowship.

Paragraph 1. Conditions for Ordination

The conditions for ordination shall be the following:

* has an adequate knowledge on Unitarianism and Universalism
* has exemplary leadership and is knowledgeable about the Unitarian Universalist Ministry
* an active member of any accredited congregation or fellowship of which such active participation may be defined on the basis of the policies of such group, otherwise if there is none, such may be defined by the church leader(s) and/or religious leader assigned
* such candidate having passed or qualified from the conditions stated above must be present in a gathering determined by the UU Ministers Association and/or the Board.

Paragraph 2. Procedures for Ordination

A recommendation letter from the office of religious leader(s) approved by the group where he/she is a member, or in accordance to its own procedures or policies of the group, must be secured by the applicant. Such letter shall be given to the President or to such person-in charge of the Unitarian Universalist Ministers Association. It shall state its reason(s) why such applicant should be ordained. The UUMA President upon receiving the application shall determine at a UUMA gathering to which the Applicant(s) shall be present for consultation and inquiries. After determining the applicant's worthiness, the President of the UUMA, shall recommend, in writing to the BOD, to be supported by other documents such as Minutes of the UUMA Meeting for such purpose, for its approval, and to the Annual Church Convention for final approval.

Section 5. The UU Ministerial Students

This section refers to those eager and interested members of the Church who wishes to undergo formal theological training at an institution that may be determined by the UU Ministers Association, the Finance & Planning

Department, the Board, and the final approval by the Annual Church Convention.

Paragraph 1. Qualification to the Ministerial Scholarship

The qualifications shall be the following:

- a high school graduate upon application
- has a good health and a good moral character
- loyal and faithful to the Unitarian Universalist Church of the Philippines, Inc.
- has been in the UUCP Statistics for the passed two years
- an active member of an accredited congregation or fellowship for the past three years
- has an adequate knowledge on the teachings of Unitarianism Universalism
- must conform and willing to serve the church as a minister after graduation.

Paragraph 2. Procedures in Applying for Ministerial Studies

The following are the procedures for applying ministerial studies:

- obtain a recommendation letter from the minister or church officer approved by the congregation or fellowship of where such applicant is a member
- submit such letter to the Scholarship Committee, a copy given to the President of the UUMA, and another copy to the Chair of the Board
- must be present during the second Board meeting for interview, and
- must be present during the following Annual Convention of which the final approval comes from

Section 6. Minister's License to Solemnize a Marriage

This section refers to Ministers who are authorized by the government of the Philippines to officiate marriage ceremonies. Such license shall only be given to Ministers who are qualified to the condition below.

Paragraph 1. Conditions to Qualify for Authority to Solemnize Marriage

- has a regular church service
- has at least twenty five (25) members
- has been in the Unitarian Universalist Association's Statistics for the past two (2) years
- has served as a Minister for a period of one (1) year after the date of ordination
- has attended a seminar on the laws and policies about solemnizing marriages conducted by the National Statistics Office

Paragraph 2. The Application Letter

The applicant must submit an application letter stating his/her desire why he/she be given a license to solemnize marriages to the President of the UU Ministers Association, who shall evaluate and recommend the applicant to the Minister's Council for further questioning. He/she must be present in such meeting of the Council, but such application shall have the final approval during the Organization's Assembly.

Section 7. Classification into Congregation or Fellowship

All churches of the Unitarian Universalist Church of the Philippines, Inc., shall be classified according to its number of active members. Such shall be that churches having twenty-five (25) members and above shall be classified as a congregation, while churches whose membership is only twenty-four (24) members below, are to be considered as fellowships.

Section 8. Definition of Active Congregation and Fellowship

Churches that are actively supportive and participative in the programs and purposes of the UUCP, Inc., shall be classified as active congregation(s) or fellowship(s).

ARTICLE XI
THE CHURCH PROPERTY

Section 1. Acquired Property

The church property are those found in the records of the church secretary as approved during the 1989 Church Convention held at the National Office, 065 Rovira Road, Bantayan, Dumaguete City, Negros Oriental, Philippines, and those properties that shall be acquired by the Church after the said Assembly.

Section 2. Congregational Property Acquired from the National Office

All acquired properties from the National Office, disseminated to all accredited congregation and fellowships shall be in custody and care by the local minister and the church officers. Upon the order of the Board with the approval by the Annual Church Convention, such properties shall be returned to the National Office.

Section 3. Place of Storage

All properties, records of receipts shall be stored at the National Office and no member or officer shall be allowed to bring and keep the same outside the said place.

ARTICLE XII
CHURCH DISCIPLINE

Section 1. Definition

Discipline is meant to prevent and correct offenses committed in adherence to a standard of ethical conduct for moral life in order to maintain church harmony and integrity.

Section 2. Scope

Ministers, Church Leaders, Elders, Deacons and Deaconess, and Church Officers shall be subject to church discipline. Likewise the discipline for members shall be done and governed in accordance to its local rules of conduct to where he/she belongs. In regards to cases unsettled by local congregation or fellowship, such may be brought to the Committee on Pastoral Care and Counseling (CPCC) attention for further investigation and decision, if in opinion of the local Disciplinary Committee will serve better effect or solution. Such request only be upon a written request signed by the Chairperson and its members accompanied by sufficient facts of the situation (scenario) and the partial investigation conducted addressed to the Chairperson of the CPCC.

Section 3. Local Disciplinary Committee

Pursuant to Section 1 of Article X of this bylaws, discipline may be implemented based on the Local Church Rules of Conduct formulated by the Local Disciplinary Committee duly approved by the members of the congregation or fellowship. If there is unavailability of these rules of conduct from such congregation or fellowship, then they may adhere or use this Article. If desire, the Local Minister, Church Leader together with the Elders may compose the Local Disciplinary Committee who shall impose discipline if by such system the group finds it desirable.

Paragraph 1. Chairperson

The disciplinary body of the local church shall be headed by a Chairperson who shall preside and officiate disciplinary investigation and may decide for appropriate solution provided that the Committee members approve such decision. He/she can only vote to break a tie decision.

Section 4. Committee on Pastoral Care and Counseling

Members of the Unitarian Universalist Ministers Association (UUMA) shall compose the Committee on Pastoral Care and Counseling, the church disciplinary body. It shall elect its own Chairperson. Furthermore, the UUCP President shall be a member of the Committee (if not minister member) with a vote.

Paragraph 1. *Powers of the Chairperson*

The Chairperson of the Committee shall preside each meeting of the committee and shall see to it that all complaints undergo proper procedures. He/she shall only vote to break a tie decision.

Paragraph 2. *Quorum*

The majority of the entire members of the committee shall constitute a quorum.

Section 5. Classification of Immoral, Unethical and Improper Conduct

Paragraph 1. *Cases for Minimal Degrees of Discipline*

It refers to the degree of offense committed by a Minister, or a Church Officer including the Department Chairperson and Staffs for nagging or gossiping, and an undesirable display of alcoholism, gambling or smoking behavior resulting to an unethical and improper conduct.

Paragraph 2. *Cases for an Advice for a Complete Withdrawal*

It refers to an unethical action committed by a Minister including Department Chairperson, Staffs and members which is against the law of the land and of God which are written as follows: Graft & Corruption, Domestic Violence, Robbery, Forgery, Rape, Murder, Drug Addiction, Adultery/Concubinage, Arson, Homicide, and Kidnapping.

Section 6. Discipline for Organizational Presidents and Officers

Presidents, Officers, and members of an organization shall be disciplined in accordance to the discipline rendered to church officers stipulated in this Article when there are no policies, rules or provision for discipline stated in their organizational bylaws.

Section 7. Written Complaint

In cases where a verbal complaint has been presented to a Minister, Congregation Officer, a Church Leader or Church Officer as the case may apply, which said alleged offender is accused of immoral, unethical or improper conduct and the same is a Minister, Church Leader, Elder, Deacon or Deaconess or Church Officers, shall be asked to lay down in writing with some specifications of time space, situation and person involved for reasons of formality and for the basis of the consultation and discussion to be made.

Gossips and rumors shall be discouraged and shall not be a basis for an inquiry. Only written complaints shall be entertained by the Committee.

Section 8. Action of the Complaint

After receiving a written complaint with all the sufficient necessary, the name(s) of the complainant(s) and the alleged offender(s), time, place, and the Scenario that constitute the immoral, unethical or improper conduct, the Committee shall seek a private consultation with the alleged offender(s) to inform him/her/them of the charge(s) in a tactful and humane manner as possible in order to ascertain his/her /their reactions and behavior. The complainant(s) may be present in such consultation, if necessary.

If the alleged offender(s) admits the truth, imposition of appropriate, just decision be rendered considering the circumstances of admission by the offender(s). But in cases where the alleged offender(s) does not admit to the facts presented or admits to some, but with some justifying expressions, then the Committee after a thorough deliberation may result to the process of reconciliation only when the complainant is present in such gathering of for counseling or through Amicable Agreement from both parties to settle the dispute, as the case may apply.

However, if the alleged offender(s) alleged of a serious offense which constitute to a violation of the laws of the land, such proceeding may be suspended to give way for appropriate legal actions and prosecution by the state authorities. Committee proceeding may resume its inquiry after the deliberation may administer a decision to maintain the integrity of church discipline. State prosecution finding(s) may be used as a basis for appropriate action.

Section 9. Reference of a Decision

Paragraph 1. Counseling

It is of greatest aspiration for a complete change or renewal or transformation of behavior or attitude of an offender(s) particularly to the first time offender(s). Counseling should be done through procedure(s) and program(s) adopted by the Committee handled by selected individuals as may be determined by the Committee.

Paragraph 2. Amicable Agreement

It is an agreement where both parties will faithfully adhere and follow to the agreed conditions formulated in a document in order to attain a peace of mind or settlement of the dispute as a way of protecting individual rights for a just decision.

Paragraph 3. Suspension

It is applied to Church Leaders, Church Officers, Department Chair and Staff members and National Committees who committed immoral, unethical or improper display of conduct while waiting for an appropriate decision.

Likewise, suspensions of Ministers shall be the temporary cancellation of his/her authority to officiate marriages and or the right to officiate religious ceremonies.

Paragraph 4. *Termination*

After due deliberation of the complaint, a church leader, church officer, elders, deacons, deaconess, department chairperson, and staff member and national committee member, and chair shall be terminated from his/her position, office or religious function/ordination after being found guilty of any immoral, unethical, or improper display of conduct. If in the best opinion of the disciplinary committee such endangers the harmony and integrity of the Church. Termination may also refer to the cancellation or rebuking of the Authority to solemnize marriage or their Ordination to the Ministry as a whole.

Paragraph 5. *Expulsion*

Any member with or without a position, office or religious ordination may be expelled from the membership of the Church if, and only if, a point of inequity was made in a just proceedings, and to the opinion of the Committee such shall serve for the best interest of the Church, then expulsion may be rendered as a decision.

ARTICLE XIII
NOMINATION AND ELECTION

Section 1. Elective Positions

The elective positions of the Church shall be the National Officers (excluding the Financial Secretary) seats, Department Chairpersons, and the Director-at-Large position. Organizational Presidents shall be elected by the Assembly of such Organization.

Section 2. Election Rules and Regulations

No person shall file a certificate for candidacy to any of the elective positions if he/she is not a member of any accredited congregation or fellowship; does not reside in the Philippines; does not have the time to serve the office, and when he or she is absent, meaning such person is not in the place and time of which the election is being done. No person can file for candidacy for more than one (1) elective position.

Section 3. Conduct of Election

This section is referring to the election by ballot and those persons who are entitled to vote.

Paragraph 1. Election by Ballot

Voting shall be written ballot. In cases where only one person has validly been selected, such person must achieve fifty percent plus one (50%+1) consensus of votes of all certified delegates in such gathering declared quorum.

Paragraph 2. Persons Entitled to Vote

Ballots shall only be cast by certified delegates of the Annual Church Convention.

Section 4. Supervision of the Election

The Secretary of the Church and the Finance and Planning Committee shall supervise all elections for elective positions. The Secretary of the Committee may designate sub-committee of tellers to count the ballots and perform other election routine duties.

Section 5. Additional Rules for Nominations and Elections

Additional rules relating to nomination and election procedures may be made by the Secretary, Finance & Planning Committee, and/or the Board, subject to the approval of the Annual Church Convention.

Section 6. Definition of Majority

The term majority shall be defined as the fifty plus one (50%+1) of all certified delegates, and all accredited congregations or fellowships in such named gathering or as the case may apply.

ARTICLE XIV
THE RULES

This Article authorizes the Board to make and implement rules and policies, which are needed for the management of all the affairs of the church, subject to the final approval of the Annual Church Convention. Such rule(s) or policy(ies) could be adopted and be part in these bylaws, if desired.

ARTICLE XV
THE AMENDMENTS

The term refers to the additions and/or changes of the content of these bylaws.

Section 1. Vote Required

These bylaws may be amended by a majority vote of all certified delegates, from the majority of all accredited congregations and fellowships present in such gathering declared quorum.

Section 2. Procedures to Amend

All amendments of these bylaws shall be done in writing, stating its reason(s) why there's a need to amend and such intention shall be presented during the Board Meeting, before such proposed amendments be made as one of the agenda of the Annual Church Convention. Such proponent must be present during the declaration of such provision in that Annual Convention.

Printed in the Negros Island, Philippines

By heritage, the Unitarian Universalist Church of the Philippines, Inc., is Universalist. Through the Securities and Exchange Commission, the Universalist Church of the Philippines was registered by the Republic of the Philippines in April 25, 1955. In 1972, the Universalist church of the Philippines was a member of the International Association for Religious Freedom in Frankfurt, Germany. In 1985, the Universalist Church of the Philippines became the Unitarian Universalist Church of the Philippines, Inc., and was registered by the Securities and Exchange Commission last January 8, 1985. The S.E.C. Registered Number of the UUCP is 124245.

In 1988, the Unitarian Universalist Church of the Philippines became a member society of the Unitarian Universalist Association and in 1995, it became a member of the International Council of Unitarian and Universalist.

Appendix 4

Unitarian Universalist Congregations
of the Philippines

1. UU Fellowship of Antol
Bulata, Cauayan
Negros Occidental

2. UU Fellowship of Aranda
Hinigaran
Negros Occidental

3. UU Church of Banaybanay
Bayawan, Santa Catalina
Negros Oriental

4. UU Church of Benejiwan
Salvador Benedicto
Negros Occidental

5. UU Church of Bugnay
Mabinay
Negros Oriental

6. UU Fellowship of Bunga
Salvador Benedicto
Negros Occidental

7. UU Church of Cabigohan
San Carlos City
Negros Occidental

8. UU Church of Caican
Santa Catalina
Negros Oriental

9. UU Church of Cama
Cama, Siaton
Negros Oriental

10. UU Church of Samaca Village
Canlaon City
Negros Oriental

11. UU Fellowship of Cansauro
Sipalay
Negros Occidental

12. UU Church of Culipapa
Hinoba-an
Negros Occidental

13. UU Fellowship of Dumaguete
065 Rovira Road, Bantayan, Dumaguete City
Negros Oriental

14. UU Church of Inapugan
Binalbagan
Negros Occidental

15. UU Church of Kalomboyan
Bayawan
Negros Oriental

16. UU Church of Kansay-an
Kansay-an, Quezon, San Carlos City
Negros Occidental

17. UU Church of Malingin
Bago City
Negros Occidental

18. UU Church of Nagbinlod
Santa Catalina
Negros Oriental

19. UU Fellowship of Nataban
San Carlos City
Negros Occidental

20. UU Church of Punong
Bayawan
Negros Occidental

21. UU Church of Samoyaw
Pamplona
Negros Oriental

22. UU Fellowship of San Rafael
Hinoba-an
Negros Occidental

23. UU Fellowship of Santol
Binalbagan
Negros Occidental

24. UU Fellowship of Tambacan
Santa Catalina
Negros Oriental

25. UU Church of Tampaga
Mantikil, Siaton
Negros Oriental

26. UU Fellowship of Valladolid
Doldol, Villadolid
Negros Occidental

Appendix 5

The Story of Toribio Quimada
and Universalism
in the Philippines:
A Church School Curriculum

By

Margaret K. Gooding

Rebecca Quimada Sienes

Contents

Introduction

Session 1: Unitarian Universalist Children in the Philippines

Session 2: Toribio Wishes for a Bible

Session 3: Three Pioneers of Universalism

Session 4: A Real Friendship

Session 5: The Bag Carrier

Session 6: On to the University

Session 7: Wider Horizons

Session 8: Preparing for the Fiesta

Session 9: Fiesta!

Biko Recipe

Song
"Maglipay Universalist"

Introduction

Goals:

This curriculum has two main goals, intertwined with each other. One is to tell the story of Toribio Sabandija Quimada, the other to present the two main ideas in Universalism as Toribio Quimada experienced them, impartiality and questioning.

Structure of the Sessions:

The structure remains the same for the first seven sessions:

1. *An activity for the children when they arrive*

> This will vary in length depending on the program of church or fellowship.

2. *An introduction to the story*

> This relies on the children's own experiences and/or thoughts.

3. *The story*

> The life of Toribio Quimada

4. *Activities that relate to the story in some way*

5. *Closing circle*

> This includes a chalice lighting, a review of the main concepts of the morning, and the singing of "Maglipay Universalist."

> The last two Sundays are devoted to the fiesta and its preparation.

A dramatization of Toribio Quimada's life is included.

What children eight to eleven years old are like:

In the Philippines both boys and girls are engaged in after school activities on which the family depends. There are no indoor bathrooms, public libraries, telephones. There is no health insurance. Both boys and girls embroider. Unitarian Universalist children generally live on farms and not in the cities.

North American girls and boys in Unitarian Universalist churches and fellowships are more apt to be urban, though some do live on farms. Their tasks at home are seldom something on which the family depends. Homes have indoor bathrooms. The children's lives are full of television, public libraries, telephones and very often computers.

In spite of these cultural differences, Filipino children and North American girls and boys living in the United States and Canada are very much alike. First and foremost they are active. In varying degrees according to their individual differences they like games, sports, drama and art. Some like to sing and others do not. Concepts of times past and places far away are developing with eight year olds and are reasonably advanced by the time they are eleven. As a rule boys like to be with boys and girls with girls. Team games are popular. Boisterous behavior is common. Keep these factors in mind when planning your sessions. The key is to keep the group active and avoid lengthy presentations or explanations. These children can take on some responsibilities. The habit of putting away materials, washing paint brushes, throwing away scraps in a waste basket . . . all of the general "leaving the room in good order tasks" . . . is something to be established at the very first session. You can enhance the children's sense of responsibility and ownership of their classroom space by occasionally remarking on how nice the room looks when they leave, and how glad you are you didn't have to do it all by yourself. But don't overdo it. Children are quick to recognize when they are being manipulated by too much praise!

Teaching:

A consistent teacher or teachers for the nine sessions works best. If you must have different people it is crucial that there be communication during the week so that the new teacher will know what happened at the last session and what the routines are.

Arrive fifteen or twenty minutes early to have everything in readiness. Plan ahead so that you will not be looking frantically for supplies and materials at the last minute.

Try out unfamiliar art projects in advance so you will know how to do them.

Give the children opportunities to question, argue, and debate, as did Toribio Quimada. Our responses and those of other children help the questioner think about his/her current ideas and thus contribute to his/her religious growth and learning.

If you do not have a room in which you can leave supplies and materials, put everything in an easily portable box that has the handles cut out. The top is open.

Stories:

The stories are much better told than read. Do not try to memorize them word for word. Read each to yourself, jot down key ideas, practice telling them aloud. If you find the stories too long for your particular group of children, decide what you can leave out and still get the main concept across.

Some words are probably beyond the children's experience. "Impartiality" and "excommunicated" are two of these. They are defined within the context of the stories but you need to make sure they are understood by the children. Do not omit them!

Books on life in the Philippines:

Filipino Unitarian Universalist boys and girls live mainly on farms and not in urban areas. Search out books that depict this. Rice fields, sugar plantations, caraboa, etc. In Canada and the United States search these out in the local library, possibly purchasing some in a book store. In the Philippines you will need to search further. In North America these books and any pictures you can find serve to acquaint class members with life on the islands. In the Philippines children can identify with the lives of the children depicted and discover how their lives are like or unlike those in the books and pictures. Include story books!

Songs:

If you sing you may not need a song leader, but if you do not be sure to find one, at least for the first two or three sessions! Then the children will know the songs well enough to take over.

A way of teaching "Maglipay Universalist" is included in the lesson plans and the two songs are also part of this curriculum. The current Unitarian Universalist hymn book, "Singing the Living Tradition," has another of Toribio Quimada's hymns . . . number 182, "O the Beauty in a Life," sung to a Visayan folk tune. More complicated than "Maglipay Universalist" you might read the words to the class and ask them what they think they mean. You might also post the words on the flip chart. Do not spend a long time on this hymn!

Supplies:

You will need the following general supplies:

- A good map of the Philippine Islands
- Drawing paper, colored construction paper
- Scissors, crayons, pencils
- Glue or glue sticks, or paste with applicators
- Staples or thumb tacks, masking tape
- Chalice, candle, matches
- Flip chart or chalk board

Other supplies needed for only a session or two are noted in each lesson. Bibles, one for each two children, are needed for Session 2.

Hello and good-bye:

If you are teaching this curriculum in the United States or Canada you might like to greet each child with "Kumosta ka," and say good-bye with "Tutuloy na ho kami." These are "hello" and "good-bye" in Tagalog. Children usually enjoy speaking another language.

Flexibility:

The Reverend Susan Manker-Seale offers the following suggestions for making this curriculum or any other work for you.

1. Things to remember about curricula:

- Curricula are designed to help us get across certain ideas, values, history, and so on. Keep this in mind.
- Curricula must be adapted to fit the many different situations and people who wish to use them.
- Be brave. Cut and paste.
- Curricula contain the best activities and suggestions that the authors could design to teach the subject. You may have better ones for your group.

2. Compare your limitations with the curriculum requirements:

- Length of meeting time: Delete or shorten activities, or lengthen them by adding other resources.
- Fluctuating attendance: Plan for the most number of children, but honor the time when there is only one because the one to one relationship is very special for both of you. Cut activities into segments that stand alone. Include review time each Sunday.
- Age range of children: If adapting down to a younger age choose more hands-on activities to convey the theme. If

adapting up involve children in choosing activities that interest them but reinforce the theme.

3. Problems teachers face and a suggested Band-Aid:

- You've finished the lesson and there's still fifteen minutes left: Always have back-up activities but ask the children what they'd like to do. Try to give choices.
- The class time is over and you've only done half the lesson: Take a minute to summarize and then proceed with your closing. This often happens when the children are really getting into the topic or activity—a "good" class. Evaluate the length of the activities you're choosing and see if it is possible to divide them into shorter segments.
- The children don't seem interested. They keep bringing up other subjects or look bored: See if you can give them choices in topics and activities so that they feel involved. Listen and see if this is a time when you need to drop the lesson and be there for them (not the same as allowing them to "take over").

Enjoy the children, your teaching, and the course!

Session 1: Unitarian Universalist Children in the Philippines

Focus:

Life on a Filipino farm
What the next eight sessions are about

What you will need:

- Song leader
- Words to "Planting Rice" and first verse of "Maglipay Universalist" on a flip chart or chalk board
- Map of the Philippines
- Drawing paper
- Crayons or paints
- Scissors
- Glue or paste and applicators
- "Biko," or a rice pudding, made at home
- Serving dishes, spoons, etc.

When the children arrive:

Talk with them about their homes and families:
Who lives at their house or apartment?
What work do parents or other adults do?
What work do children do?
Are there pets?
If the children do not know each other, ask each to give his/her name before they tell about their homes and families.

To introduce the story:

In the Philippines: Ask the children to listen carefully to discover what is the same and what is different in their lives and that of Manuel and Estella.

In Canada and the United States: This first story is about a Unitarian Universalist girl and boy on their family farm in the Philippines. Show the map of the Philippine Islands. Help the children find Cebu. Ask them to listen carefully to the story to discover what is the same and what is different in the lives of Manuel and Estella from their own.

Story: "At Home on the Island of Cebu"

The kerosene lamps were lit. The supper of rice and beans had been eaten. The children were munching on cashews. Outside the house the dogs stood guard against any robbers, and inside the cats were watching for any mice that might be on the lookout for a dropped cashew nut or a grain of rice that had fallen to the floor. It was a Friday evening and Manuel and Estella were a bit sleepy. Still, they had lots to tell about their day at school.

"My side won the tug-of-war," Manuel said, "and when we played baseball we won that, too."

Estella spoke up. "I think soccer is more fun than baseball," she said. "You get to play all the time and don't have to wait so long for your turn."

Estella was not very good at waiting, and indeed Manuel wasn't either. Their parents were very interested in what happened at school.

"You must have done other things besides play games outside," said their father. "What did you learn inside the school house?"

"Well, some of us took turns reading a story about how a firefly got the better of some apes. And I only made one mistake multiplying those numbers by four. I learned that a lot of pineapples grow on the Hawaiian Islands. I learned that in the United States in the state of Iowa they grow corn, but they can't grow it all year because some of the time it snows. I wondered what snow is like. I learned that Manila is the capital of the Philippine Islands, and Washington of the United States and Ottawa of Canada. I learned that here in the Philippine Islands the government protects animals that are endangered. One of the animals is the tamaraw.

"I learned how to say 'good-bye' in Tagalog, which is the official language of the Philippine Islands. I know that we speak Cebuano here on Cebu, so that when we say 'good-bye' we say 'adto na mi,' but in Tagalog it is 'tutuloy na ho kami.' Hello is the same in both languages though, 'kumosta ha'!"

Estella and Manuel kept interrupting each other as they told what happened that day in school. The public school they went to was about four kilometers away (almost two and a half miles) and it was a long walk! As they talked they began to get sleepier and sleepier. It was time for bed. Off they went to the outdoor bathroom and then into their beds for the night.

On Saturday they were up bright and early, for there was lots to do around the farm.

All kinds of vegetables grow in the rich soil: squash, eggplant, lettuce, cabbage, beans, malunggay (horse radish), corn, and of course the rice which grows in the watery fields. Manuel and Estella helped keep the garden free of weeds. They fed the chickens and the hogs. They climbed up the banana tree so each could pick and eat a ripe banana. They checked the corn in the corn field and brought their mother a dozen ripe ears so they could have corn-on-the-cob for supper.

In the middle of the hot afternoon their mother called to them and said, "I think you had better take your school clothes down to the river and wash them. While you're there you can have a good swim and wash yourselves too."

Swimming in the river was such fun that they almost forgot about washing the clothes, but Estella made sure they did that too.

Spread out on the grass and bushes the clean clothes dried very quickly. It was time to go home. Supper was ready!

The corn-on-the-cob tasted really good. After supper Manuel and Estella settled down to do a bit of embroidery, for at school both boys and girls are taught to embroider.

It had been a busy day. Estella and Manuel were sleepy, so after another trip to the outdoor bathroom they went to bed, listening to the rain on the palm leaf roof of their log and bamboo home.

On Sunday they would go to the village to their Unitarian Universalist Sunday School. On Monday, back to the public school again.

Discussion:

In the Philippines: Give the children an opportunity to tell how their lives are like and how they are different from Manuel and Estella's.

In the United States and Canada: What do Estella and Manuel do that is the same as the class members do? What is different? Help them say "hello" and "good-bye" in Tagalog.

Activity I: Dramatizing the words to "Planting Rice"

Notes for the leader: The best way to teach these words to children this age is to say each phrase and then have the children say it with you. Then everyone say it all the way through two or three times.

The phrases:

1. Planting rice is never fun
2. Bent from morn 'til set of sun
3. Cannot stand and cannot sit
4. Cannot rest for a little bit
5. Planting rice is no fun/Bent from morn 'til set of sun
6. Cannot stand cannot sit/Cannot rest for a little bit

Activity II: Eating the "Biko"

Pictures of the children's homes

Have the paper, crayons and/or paints, scissors, glue or paste available. Give out the pudding, which the children eat while you talk about the pictures they will make about their homes.

Where are their homes located?

Of what are they made?

Who lives there?

What does it look like on the outside?

Are there trees, flowers, plants?

In the Philippines each child makes a picture of his/her home.

In Canada and the United States discuss with the children what is different about the Filipino home and their homes.

Suggest that each make a picture of the outside of his/her home.

Leave time for them to share their pictures. Be sure to thank each child.

Again, if the children are not acquainted with each other, have them tell who they are before they share their pictures. You will need to tell your name and have a picture of your home to share!

Closing circle:

Gather the children in a circle and light the chalice. If they are not already familiar with the chalice you may need to explain its significance. There are a number of interpretations. Probably the best one for this age is that the chalice is the circle of friendship and the light the quest for new knowledge.

This will lead you into an explanation of the next eight Sundays. The children are going to learn about Toribio Quimada and how he brought Universalism, which became Unitarian Universalism, to the Philippine Islands. There will be a story each Sunday, arts and craft projects, and play acting. The last Sunday will be a fiesta.

Sing "Maglipay Universalist" as a closing song. The words on the flip chart or chalkboard will help.

Choose one child to extinguish the chalice.

Session 2: Toribio Wishes for a Bible

Focus:

Toribio Quimada's wish to read a Bible. In it he believes he will find answers to his religious questions.

What you will need:

- Words to the second verse of "Maglipay Universalist" printed on a flip chart or chalkboard
- Bibles, one for every two children
- Materials for pictures of "hell"
- Drawing paper
- Crayons, felt tip markers, or poster paints and brushes— with plenty of reds and yellows
        and/or
- Red and yellow construction paper
- Glue or paste and applicators
- Scissors
- Black or gray construction paper for mounting
- Pictures and picture books of life in the Philippines
- Map of the Philippine Islands

As the children arrive:

Invite them to browse among the pictures and picture books.

To introduce the story:

Engage the children in a conversation about the concepts of heaven and hell. Are they real places? Do people today think they are real places? Encourage the children to present their own ideas without criticism but with opportunities for discussion. Do not let the conversation go on for too long! To close the conversation say something like . . . today's story is about Toribio Quimada, a man who lived in the Philippines and who didn't believe anyone would go to hell forever. He believed he would find proof of this in the Bible, but it was a long time before he was allowed to read one.

Story: "Toribio's Wish"

Toribio Quimada had wanted to own and read a Bible for a very long time.

"God must be a loving God," he thought. "God would never punish anyone forever and ever. If I could only read what it says about God in the Bible I know that's what I would find."

Toribio was a teenager when he had these thoughts, but he was twenty years old before he had an opportunity to find out what the Bible says.

He was born on the island of Cebu in the Philippines. His father, Zolio, a farmer and a carpenter, was Spanish in origin, his mother a mixture of Spanish and Malay. There was no Bible in Zolio's home, for it was forbidden by the very strict and powerful religion to which most of the people on the island belonged. Zolio believed without question what his church taught him. He expected his wife and children to do the same. No asking questions about what the church taught! If anyone outside the family questioned or criticized Zolio's beliefs he became very angry and challenged that person to a fist fight.

Still, Toribio had questions, though he did not expect answers from his father. If only he had a Bible, for he thought the Bible would tell him what he wanted to know.

God was supposed to be a loving God, why would God condemn some people to hell forever? Wasn't God supposed to be impartial and love everyone equally? Does the Bible really say we should pray to a statue of Mary, Jesus' mother? How could God be Jesus' father? Wasn't Joseph his father? These were some of Toribio's questions, the most important one, wasn't God supposed to be impartial and love everyone equally?

Toribio's father didn't think much of education. He wanted his children to be able to write well enough to write a letter. He wanted them to be able to read well enough to understand the ballot so they could vote, but that was all. Education as a way of learning about the world, of changing some ideas was not what he believed education was for! Toribio and his brothers and sisters worked in the family's garden, herded the livestock, pulled weeds and planted rice. He did go to school to learn to read and write, but not until he was ten years old. It was the Minglanilla School in the village and he went there for only six years. He wanted to grow up to be a lawyer but there wasn't enough money for that kind of education.

It was because there wasn't enough money to be made on the farm that the whole Quimada family moved to San Carlos City and into the home of Zolio's brother, Fernando. And there in Fernando's home Toribio's wish came true! He got to read the Bible! Fernando was of different faith than Zolio. His religion allowed the Bible to be read and not only that, he opened Toribio's eyes to finding out about other faiths.

Toribio wrote, "After a long period of waiting and longing, the time has come for me to read this precious book, the Holy Bible. This is the most valuable possession I ever had and will ever be in my life. Through this I will learn the story about the Prophets, Patriachs, Apostles, and Jesus Christ.

He studied the Bible carefully and in it discovered passages which proclaimed God's impartiality. God loved everyone equally!

> Psalm 145:9   The lord is good to all and his tender mercies are over all his works.
> I John 4:8   God is love.
> James 3:17   The wisdom that is from above . . . is without partiality.
> I Timothy 2:3,4 . . . God . . . will have all men be saved.

Still, he didn't find quite the right church. He left the church in which he grew up and began to attend the closest one he could find, Iglesia Universal de Christo. As you can imagine this made his father very angry. He would challenge Toribio, now in his twenties, to a debate about the beliefs of his new faith. It didn't matter who was in the house, family or friends.

Toribio still had many questions that his new faith did not answer. He was a "critic, rather than a good Christian and a faithful follower of Jesus Christ." Nevertheless he was asked to teach Sunday School and do some preaching. Seven years after the family moved to San Carlos City the whole Quimada family, including Toribio's wife, Sergia and even his father, Zolio, joined the Iglesia Universal de Christo. Five years after that Toribio was ordained as one of their ministers. He became a circuit-rider, going to churches in nine different villages, usually many kilometers from each other. He walked all the way.

The questions he had, however, remained unanswered. One of the things that bothered him was why the Iglesia Universal de Christo did not have its own religious education materials. He had to use those from other faiths for the Sunday School classes he taught. He didn't like that!

His question was, "How can a church not be able to provide its own religious (education) materials for its own use?"

Toribio had found a faith much more to his liking, but it still wasn't quite right. Universalism still hadn't come to the Philippines.

Activity I: A Bible Search

We talk about the Bible with our Unitarian Universalist boys and girls but seldom do we put one in their hands. It is important that they have some direct experience with this collection of books that is so significant in our culture, whether it be Filipino, Canadian, or American. Begin this activity by finding out what the children already know about the Bible. Use your understanding of the group as well as what you know has been the content of their church school classes to determine how much additional information to give them. Too much will turn them off, too little will confuse them.

The Bible is a collection of books written by many different authors at many different times. The Old Testament, or more correctly the Hebrew Scriptures, is the story of the Jews before the time of Jesus. The New Testament is the story of Jesus' life . . . as told by Matthew, Mark, Luke and John . . . and of Jesus' teachings and his followers.

Give the children time to explore the Bible, to comment and ask questions. Why do they think the Old Testament is so much longer than the New Testament? (The time period is much longer.) What does "testament" mean? (In this instance it refers to the two main divisions of the Christian Bible.) What does epistle mean? (A letter.) The last book, Revelation, describes what long ago Christians thought the end of the world would be like.

If the Bibles the children have do not include the Apocrypha (an addition to the Jewish and Protestant Bibles included in the Roman Catholic Bible), ask the children to hold the Bible on its spine and open it up in the middle. This should be the Psalms and the back cover is the book of Matthew, the beginning of Jesus' story.

What did Toribio Quimada find in the Bible? What did it tell him about God's impartiality? (Do the children understand what "impartiality" means?) Help the children find the following passages, making sure they understand that the first number following the name of the book tells the chapter, and the next number or numbers the verse.

Psalm 145:9   The Lord is good to all and his tender mercies are over all his works.
I John 4:8   God is love.

James 3:17   The wisdom that is from above . . . is
without partiality.
      I Timothy 2:3,4 . . . God . . . will have all men be saved.

Discuss with the children what these verses meant to
Toribio Quimada.

Activity II: Imaginative pictures of "hell"

Invite the children to use their imagination to make
pictures of what people who believed in "hell" thought it
looked like. Provide the materials in a central place and
give free rein to the children's ideas. They may wish to
share their pictures when finished. If so, emphasize the
imaginary ideas of their concepts.
      A good question to ask, "Do any people believe in hell
today?"

Closure:

Light the chalice.
      Introduce the second verse of "Maglipay Universalist"
in either Filipino or English. The tune is a Filipino folk
song. The words are by Toribio Quimada.
      Close by singing "Maglipay Universalist."
      Choose one child to extinguish the chalice.

Session 3: Three Pioneers of Universalism

Focus:

The right of everyone to criticize, ask questions, and
sometimes change their minds.

What you will need:

- A globe or world map
- Words to the second verse of "Maglipay Universalist" on
  a flip chart or chalk board
- Something to resemble a wood pile (You may want to
  bring in a few fireplace logs.)
- Something to resemble a padlocked church door
  (Can you provide a padlock and hasp?)

- A newspaper
- A sheet of writing paper
- An almanac
- Copies of curricula recently used in the church school

As the children arrive:

Help them find the Philippines, Wisconsin, New Hampshire, Lake Winnipeg in Manitoba Canada, Iceland, and Boston, Massachusetts on the globe or map.

Have the pictures and picture books of the Philippines available for browsing.

Have the copies of recent curricula available for browsing.

To introduce the three stories:

Say something like . . . Universalism as a recognized religion began in the United States in the late 1700's, over two hundred years, ago. It was a long time, however, before it became known in other parts of the world. In the Philippine Islands it was barely fifty years ago that it became known, when your grandparents were small children. I am going to tell you three stories, about three people who asked questions, looked things up in books, and were willing to change their minds. They believed in the authority of truth, known or to be known. We'll stop after each story and act it out. The three people are Universalist pioneers.

The stories and their dramatizations:

Hosea Ballou

Hosea put the book he was reading in among the logs in the woodpile. His father was coming out of the house and he looked angry, really angry. He looked at Hosea and asked him, "What book are you reading there?"

Hosea answered, "A Universalist book."

"You know I don't want you reading any Universalist books," was his father's retort as he stormed back into the house.

Hosea went about his farm chores. When he had disappeared from sight his father, whose name was Maturin Ballou, came back out of the house and went over to the woodpile to retrieve the book. It was a Bible!

The year was 1789, over two hundred years ago. Most people in that part of the world, one of the states in the United States called New Hampshire, were Calvinists. They believed that no matter how blamelessly they lived God had decided before they were born that when they died many of them would go to hell and stay there forever. This bothered Hosea. When he was around eighteen years old he began to read the Bible very carefully. In those long ago days farming people in Canada and the United States had almost no books, but one they did have was a Bible. What Hosea discovered as he read was that God was a loving father. Hosea became convinced that such a God would never condemn anyone to hell forever. God promised universal salvation, hence the name Universalist. Universal means all.

Maturin Ballou, a minister at another faith, never agreed with Hosea but nevertheless loved him very much. He probably felt sad when Hosea began to preach Universalism but he knew it was Hosea's decision and it didn't affect Maturin's love. Father Hosea is what Hosea came to be called. He was one of the founders of Universalism.

To dramatize Hosea's story:

Ask for volunteers to be Hosea Ballou and his father, Maturin. With the children's help, set the scene.

Magnus Skaptason

In 1890, one hundred and one years later, another person discovered and preached Universalism in a part of the world that had not heard of it.

On the western shore of Lake Winnipeg in the province of Manitoba in Canada a man named Magnus Skaptason trudged along the muddy roads going south toward the little settlement of Gimli. He stopped along the way to preach in the churches of other small villages. It was spring in a land where there is snow and the ground is frozen all winter. The frozen ground was melting and becoming muddy, very muddy. Magnus had started out on his horse but the horse had soon become mired in the mud so Magnus was on foot.

Magnus was really a minister, but of another faith and he was supposed to preach that anyone who did not believe what his church taught would burn in hell forever. Magnus just did not believe that. The God he read about in the Bible was a loving father, and surely no loving father would punish his children forever and ever. And what about all the people in Africa, in Australia, the Americas, Asia, and in Europe who believed differently. What about Jesus?

Magnus thought, "Where is there hatred in the life of Jesus? He healed the sick, gave bread to the hungry, comforted those who were sad. He could not have preached being in hell forever, eternal damnation."

This is what Magnus talked about from the pulpit all the way down the west side of Lake Winnipeg from the island of Heckla to the village of Gimli. It is called his "Break Away" sermon because in it he broke away from his old beliefs. When he got to Gimli the church doors were padlocked against him. Those in charge had heard about his ideas. They called it heresy because it went against what they believed and taught. It was time he was stopped! However, most of the people up and down the west side of Lake Winnipeg who heard Magnus liked what he said, and they too "broke away" from their old beliefs. They formed the Icelandic Conference. They had all come to Canada from Iceland, Magnus too, and they valued both fairness and thinking for themselves. They believed in salvation for everyone.

To dramatize Magnus's story:

Ask for volunteers to be Magnus Skaptason and two or three to be those in charge in Gimli. The other children can be those to whom Skaptason spoke on his way down

Lake Winnipeg, and those who agreed with him in Gimli.
With the children's help, set the scene.

Toribio Sabandija Quimada
   In another part of the world, the Philippine Islands,
Universalism was not heard of for a very long time.
Toribio Quimada was thirty one years old and one of the
ministers of the Iglesia Universal de Christo. It was 1951.
He had been asked to baptize a newly born infant. The letter asking him to do this had come wrapped up in an old
newspaper to keep it from being damaged. Toribio looked at
the newspaper and discovered to his surprise that it listed
the religions in the United States. He hoped to find Iglesia
Universal de Christo, which wasn't there, but what he did
find was the Universalist Church of Wisconsin.
   He wrote, "This is my first time to meet such a word
(as) 'Universalist'. What is this? I was perplexed and puz-
zled over the similarities in the two words 'Universal' and
'Universalist'. I cannot understand the warmth inside me,
thus, I contemplated deeply the meaning of this word."
   He sent a letter to the Universalist Church of Wisconsin but it was returned "Addressee Unknown." He was dis-
appointed, for he was not entirely happy with the beliefs
of the Iglesia Universal de Christo. Although he had become a minister of that church he questioned some of its
teachings. Not only that, it didn't supply its own Sunday
School materials! Some months after his letter to Wisconsin was returned a friend handed him an almanac, and
there again was a listing of the churches in the United
States, among them the Universalist Church of Gloucester, Massachusetts. Again he wrote a letter, and this time
he received an answer!
   The minister of the church, Carl Westman, was surprised to receive a letter from such a far away place as the
Philippines. He forwarded Toribio's letter to the Reverend
Carleton M. Fisher of the Universalist Service Committee
who corresponded with Toribio Quimada for two years.
The Universalist Church of America, through the efforts
of Carleton Fisher and then the Reverend Dana Klotzle,

supplied Toribio Quimada with religious education materials and other items.

Rev. Quimada wrote, "This made me and my church
members happy because there are materials for children
as well as for adults."

Toribio Quimada had found a religion in which he
could believe. He preached that a loving God is not capable of preparing a place called hell for people to be tormented forever with fire. He preached that the
contradictions found in the Bible is proof that the Holy
Bible is not the word of God but an inspired book written
by inspired people. He preached that Jesus Christ is not
the son of God, but rather a gifted son of Joseph and Mary,
who delivered a message of justice, equality, and compassion. He preached that it cannot be proved in any way
that Mary conceived Jesus through the Holy Spirit. Scientifically it is illogical and unfounded and against human nature.

Universalism had come to the Philippines. In 1955 the
Universalist Church of the Philippines was registered by
the Philippine Government in Manila and Toribio
Quimada was licensed as a Universalist minister. In 1985
the Universalist Church of the Philippines became the
Unitarian Universalist Church of the Philippines.

To dramatize Toribio Quimada's story:

Volunteers are needed to be Toribio Quimada, the
friend who gave him the almanac, Carl Westman, Carleton Fisher, and Dana Klotzle. With the children's help,
set the scene.

Additional activity:

If there is time left in the session, engage the children
in a conversation about what they have learned in their
church school sessions. What have they liked? What do
they have questions about? What has surprised them? Is
there anything about which they disagree?

Closing circle:

Light the chalice. Engage the children in a brief conversation about what is important in these three stories. If it is not mentioned, emphasize using reason and research before changing one's mind. What research did Hosea Ballou, Magnus Skaptason, and Toribio Quimada do?
Sing the second verse of "Maglipay Universalist."
Choose one child to extinguish the chalice.

Session 4: A Real Friendship

Focus:

Intercultural understanding as a way to friendship

What you will need:

- The words to the second verse of "Maglipay Universalist" on a flip chart or chalk board
- Crayons, felt markers, or poster paints and brushes
- 22 cm x 30 cm (9" x 12") drawing paper cut into 11 1/2 cm x 30 cm (4 1/2" x 12") strips for cartoons
- 22 cm x 30 cm (9" x 12") drawing paper for embroidery designs
- Optional:
  embroidery hoops, transfer paper, embroidery floss, transfer pencil, embroidery needles, embroidery design, plain handkerchiefs

As the children arrive:

Have the pictures and picture books, and the globe and map available for browsing.

To introduce the story:

Talk with the children about the games they like to play, the crafts and art projects they enjoy, their favorite stories. What do they do when not in school? In North America girls and boys go roller blading, swim, ride their bicycles, watch television, etc. In the Philippines children enjoy playing tug-of-war and hide-and-seek but they are also busy helping the parents by watching younger children, washing clothes, looking for firewood. Cultures differ! Today's story tells how the kind and cheerful Universalist theology came to the Philippines. It also tells how learning about other cultures helps friendships grow.

Story: "A Real Friendship"

"This makes me and my church members happy because there are materials for the children as well as for adults."

Toribio Quimada wrote these words after he had received religious education materials—books, hymn books, children's books—from the Universalist Church of America whose headquarters were in Boston, Massachusetts in the United States. He had been bothered that the church of which he was still a minister did not have its own Sunday School materials. Now he could teach and help others to teach something in which he wholeheartedly believed. It was really Universalist theology, which means the beliefs of the Universalist religion. The leaders of the Iglesia Universal de Christo didn't like that very much, and finally the Reverend Quimada was excommunicated. Excommunicated means that he was not allowed to be a member of that church anymore, and of course no longer one of its ministers. "Universal" to that church did not mean everyone, it only meant those who believed that Jesus was actually the son of God, however they thought that could have happened!

The Reverend Dana Klotzle had become the head of the Universalist Service Committee after the Reverend Carleton Fisher had resigned. Toribio Quimada wrote to Dana Klotzle, and Dana was very impressed with his enthusiasm for Universalism. He thought Toribio was a very remarkable man and promised to do everything he could to have the Philippine Universalist Church registered with the Philippine government. It wasn't an easy task! Toribio's preaching and teaching Universalist ideas had sparked hatred, conflict, and jealousy among the members of the Iglesia Universal de Christo. That was what got him excommunicated! To them Toribio was a heretic. These same people now tried to keep him from registering the Universalist Church of the Philippines with the Filipino government. But Toribio and Dana Klotzle were very determined and worked very hard. All the necessary documents were submitted. In 1955 the Universalist Church of the Philippines was registered with the Securities and Exchange Commission of the Republic of the Philippines, as required by the law of that country. Soon after that Toribio Quimada was licensed as a minister of the Universalist Church of the Philippines. A kind, compassionate, and cheerful theology had come to the country.

Dana wrote that he helped Toribio organize the new church in keeping with the cultural values and hopes of his people. The culture of any of the places where the Universalist Church of America tried to be of help was important. It meant paying attention to the arts, the songs, the stories, the customs of the people of that place. Universalists never went anywhere to tell the people what to do. They worked with the people to make change happen. The helping hand they gave was always an expression of their religion of love. As God loves us so must we show our love to others. Working with people instead of for them did as much for those who helped as for those in need.

The diversity of humankind was important to Dana Klotzle and his wife, Ruth. They knew that in that diversity there was a unity, a oneness. Songs and food and games might be different but they were common to everyone. Ways of expressing joy and sadness might differ, but they were feelings everyone had all over the world.

Together Ruth and Dana wrote "Friendship Programs" to be used in Universalist Church schools. Boys and girls exchanged letters with children in other places. They learned their songs and games and handicrafts. They prepared and ate their foods. They heard their stories. This happened everywhere the Universalist Service Committee went. The big term for it is "intercultural un-

derstanding." It is a way of saying, "Let's be friends."
While the grown ups were involved in making changes,
the girls and boys were learning about each other.

One of the stories told in the Philippine Islands is *The
Battle of the Firefly and the Apes*. Right away this tells you
that there are apes and fireflies on the islands! The story
goes like this:

Darkness comes very quickly to the Philippine Islands. The little lamps of the fireflies begin to glimmer
and flicker among the trees. One evening as one of the
fireflies went to visit a friend he met an ape.

"Ho, ho Mr. Firefly, why do you always carry a light
with you?" the ape wanted to know.

"So I can see the mosquitoes and keep out of their
way," was the firefly's answer.

"Keep out of the way of the mosquitoes! You're afraid
of mosquitoes? You're a coward!" cried the ape.

"No, I'm not a coward and I'm not afraid of the mosquitoes. I leave the mosquitoes alone to go their way and
I go mine," said the firefly.

"I still think you're afraid of them, retorted the ape.
The next day he told all his ape friends what a coward the
firefly was, even afraid of mosquitoes. The apes laughed
and laughed and made fun of the firefly.

The firefly heard how the apes were laughing at him
and he decided to teach them a lesson. He went to the
ape's house and found the ape fast asleep. He flashed his
lamp in the ape's face and woke him up.

"Why did you tell all your friends that I was a coward,
afraid of mosquitoes?" he asked. "Come to the plaza to-
morrow and we will prove right there and then whether
or not I am a coward."

The ape laughed. "So you're offering to fight with me?
Who are you going to bring to help you? I am such a powerful
creature one of your size can hardly stand alone against me."

"I shall come alone," was the firefly's answer.

"Come alone?" cried the ape. "I will bring a whole company of apes, each one as big as myself. We shall see what
happens if you dare to come alone."

The ape ordered each of his friends to get a club and meet him on the plaza. Only the one firefly was waiting there for them. The ape drew his company up in a line, with himself at the head. Then he ordered them to go after the firefly.

The firefly swiftly flew over and landed on the first ape's nose. The next ape in line lifted his club to squash the firefly, but the firefly flew out of reach and the club came down on the first ape's nose. Flat fell Mr. Ape to the ground! The firefly landed on the second ape's nose. The next ape in line tried to hit it, but again the firefly flew away. The club hit the second ape's nose and he too fell to the ground. And so it went, all the way down the line of apes. Each ape aimed his club at the firefly on his neighbor's nose, the firefly flew away just in time; the ape hit his neighbor's nose and knocked him flat. The firefly won all his foes.

"Now who can say the firefly is afraid?" he cried.

The apes lay on the ground, never saying a word. The firefly flew away, minding his own business as before.

(*Adapted from Miller, Olive Beaupre, My Book House III, The Book House for Children, 1948 printing, pages 59–61.*)

Activity: Art projects

1. cartoon pictures
Suggest that some of the children may like to make a cartoon of the story of the firefly and the apes. How many panels will be needed? Write the content of each on a flip chart or chalkboard. Direct the children to the strips of paper and the art supplies.

2. embroidery designs
Some children may prefer to make embroidery designs using the drawing paper and art supplies.

3. embroidery
If you have sufficient help, some children may like to try embroidery. (Many Filipino boys and girls are taught embroidery in school and may not need as much help.)

Most will need help using the hoops and transferring the design.

Two designs are included. The children may like to make their own. This is an opportunity to involve members of the congregation who know how to embroider but are not usually with the children. A one to one ratio is best! A simple outline stitch may be used, or something more complicated. Unfinished projects may be taken home, or left to be worked on when the children arrive or as an alternate project during the activity phase of the morning.

Closing circle:

Light the chalice.

Engage the children in a brief conversation about the stories and activities. Emphasize where help came from for Toribio Quimada and the new Philippine Universalists, what the children have discovered through their activities about Filipino culture. With Filipino children, what would they like boys and girls in the United States and Canada to know about them? How important were children to Toribio Quimada?

Sing the second verse of "Maglipay Universalist."

Choose one child to extinguish the chalice.

Session 5: The Bag Carrier

Focus:

The importance of questioning and discussion

What you will need:

- Words to the second verse of "Maglipay Universalist" on a flip chart or chalk board
- Easily and quickly molded materials, such as Play Dough
- Colored paper and scissors
- Paste or glue
- A table to represent the market
- A long twig, about a meter (3 feet) long
- A canvas bag with a hymn book, Bible, and raincoat in it
- Something to represent a microphone and speakers

As the children arrive:

Invite them to browse among the pictures and picture books of the Philippines. Have the globe and/or map available. Make sure there are pictures of the jungle, of the fruits and vegetables sold in the market.

To introduce the story:

Engage the children in a conversation about how their parents obtain their food. Does it grow on the farm? Do they go to a market or a big store? How do they get there? Say something like . . . Today's story is about market day in the Philippines and how difficult it was sometimes to get there. Locate Quezon on the map.

Story: "The Bag Carrier"

The bag contained a hymn book, a Bible, a raincoat, and the Reverend Quimada's lunch. The bag carrier was Rebecca Quimada, his daughter, who often traveled with Toribio. On most Saturdays Toribio, Rebecca, and others from the Universalist Church walked four miles through the jungle to Quezon, where Saturday was market day. There Toribio Quimada and some of the others would preach about Universalism to the people who had gathered there.

Quezon was about a four hour walk through the jungle from Toribio's farm home. To be there by noon everyone had to get up early. There were often flooded rivers to cross, for it rains often in the Philippines and the rivers flood easily. How could you tell if you were going to get in over your head? You used a sturdy twig from a tree, sticking it in the water to learn how deep it was and then chose the shallower way.

Market day in Quezon was a time when merchants and business men from neighboring villages came to transact business, when farmers living close by brought what they had raised to sell, when the villagers bought what they needed to feed and clothe their families. It was an exciting and busy day.

The Universalist Service Committee had provided the Reverend Quimada with a public address system. He and the others who were preaching could speak into the microphone and all over the market place their words would be heard. What did they preach about? They said salvation is for everyone, Universalism is an impartial religion. They said that hell is hatred of your neighbors and heaven is your love for them. They asked if Jesus was the son of God, or the son of Joseph and Mary. All kinds and ages of people listened to them; old people, parents, young men and women, children.

Sometimes there were leaders from other religious faiths who would question what Toribio Quimada said. Toribio liked that. Rebecca loved to listen. Questioning was important and so was discussion. It not only made ideas clearer and easier to understand, it sometimes helped people to change their minds. Toribio Quimada was always willing to have questions and a discussion after he had preached.

He was really a circuit rider, although he did not ride, he walked. Within twenty to twenty five miles of his farm were nine Universalist congregations as well as some preaching stations. (What is a preaching station?) Toribio worked hard on his farm six days a week and went out preaching on the seventh. Of course he didn't do all that by himself. Others who believed in Universalism did some of the preaching too.

Toribio Quimada encouraged questions and discussions about religious ideas from the people who listened to him. The powerful church to which most of the people belonged didn't allow that. The people loved sharing the religious ideas with the Reverend Quimada and with each other. What were their ideas about God? What did they think of the Bible? What was heaven? Was there really a hell? Although they had little or no education they were happy to share their ideas, and what was said was as good as what was said by people who had gone to the university.

Sometimes people came to him for advice about their health problems. There is no health insurance in the

Philippines and people could not always go to the cities for their medicines. Toribio had been trained as a barangay health worker. Barangay means village. Along with medical advice he always told them about Universalism. Some of them became Universalists.

Besides preaching and helping people with their health problems Toribio Quimada worked on his farm to support his wife and six children. He had seven hectares, which is about seventeen acres, of rice and corn. In the evenings when the work was done he read, translated hymns and responsive readings, composed songs and wrote balaks. A balak is a four line poem. One of his songs, O the Beauty in a Life, is number 182 in our hymn book, "Singing the Living Tradition." It is sung to a Filipino folk tune. (Look this up if hymn books are available.)

The Reverend Toribio Quimada was loved and respected by all who knew him. His daughter, Rebecca Quimada Sienes, who carried his bag when he went about preaching Universalism is now the President of the Unitarian Universalist Church of the Philippines.

Activity I: Setting up the market

List on the flip chart or chalk board some of the things that might be sold in the market. What kinds of fruits and vegetables were there? Were there chickens and hogs? Was there fish? Invite the children to use the modeling material and the colored paper to make replicas of some of the things that were for sale. Set up the market.

Activity II: The market, a dramatization

You will need someone to be Toribio Quimada, someone to be Rebecca, the merchants at the market, the audience for Toribio's sermon about Universalism. The scenes might go:

1. Going through the jungle single file with hands on the one in front of you. Toribio has the twig.
2. Circulating in the market, deciding what to buy.

3. Listening to Toribio preach.
4. Asking questions.

Closing circle:

Light the chalice.

Engage the children in a conversation about the importance of asking questions, of talking about what our religion believes, of knowing that not everyone believes the same thing. What do they think about Toribio's ideas of heaven and hell? What questions do they have about the way we do things in our church or fellowship? What do they like about coming? What makes them cross? What don't they understand?

Sing the second verse of "Maglipay Universalist."

Choose one child to extinguish the chalice.

Session 6: On to the University

Focus:

The importance of education to Toribio Quimada and to each of us

What you will need:

- Words to the second verse of "Maglipay Universalist" printed on a flip chart or chalk board
- A detailed map of the Philippine islands, included with this curriculum
- Crayons, felt markers, or poster paints and brushes
- Pictures and picture books of life in the Philippines with something new added

As the children arrive:

Help them find Dumaguete City in Negros Oriental and Calatrava in Negros Occidental. (Negros Island is divided into two provinces, Negros Oriental and Negros Occidental.)

Invite them to browse among the pictures and books about the Philippine Islands.

To introduce the story:

Talk with the children about something they were at first afraid to try but when they became brave enough to do they really enjoyed. Start with an experience of your own; for example:

"I was afraid to ride a bicycle but when I dared to try it I discovered I liked it and had fun with my friends."

Use your own example. Do not insist that everyone contribute. To close the conversation say something like . . . this week's story begins with a man who was afraid he would die if he rode a horse.

Story: "On to the University!"

"Oh no, if I get up on that horse it will be my last day on earth!" Toshio Yoshioka, a Universalist minister from Japan, was visiting Toribio Quimada. He had never been on a horse before and he was truly frightened. The horse seemed so big and besides that, it snorted. Toshio, however, was a brave man and he did go for a horseback ride. Nothing happened to him, except that he enjoyed the experience, which is often the way when we do something we are afraid of. Toshio had become a Universalist minister while in the United States and was stopping in the Philippines on his way home to Japan. He received a very warm welcome from the Philippine Universalists whom he met. He loved them and their enthusiasm for Universalism. The Philippine Universalists were trying to start Sunday Schools, using the materials sent to them by the Universalist Service Committee. He had great admiration for their efforts, knowing how important to a church are good and interesting programs for children.

When the Reverend Yoshioka returned to Japan he wrote to Dana Klotzle of the Universalist Service Committee. In his letter he recommended that funds be found to send to Toribio Quimada to Silliman University. Although Toribio Quimada read many books and was what we call "self educated," like Hosea Ballou, he had only gone so far as grade seven. Indeed, he had not quite finished that grade! This bothered him a lot, so much so that he called it "shameful"! He believed leaders should be well educated, and he was not. Quite different from his father who didn't believe education was important.

The Universalist Service Committee agreed with Toshio Yoshioka, and Toribio Quimada enrolled as a special student at Silliman University in Dumaguete City, Negros Oriental. It wasn't easy for him in spite of all the reading he had done, and besides working on his farm to support his family, Toribio was overseeing twenty two groups of Universalists in local parishes. And he didn't even have a high school education! Nevertheless, off to Silliman University he went by himself, returning to work on the farm on weekends. He wanted to be a better leader as a Universalist minister. His advisor was the vice-president of the University, Dr. Robert Silliman. Dr. Silliman wrote,

"He is getting out more on the campus, such as getting a lot of new ideas that will be of value to him when he returns to his work than he would have known had he not come here . . . he will undoubtedly have (also) acquired a number of new sermon topics."

Toribio was labeled as a "trouble maker" when he was at Silliman University. He debated, he argued, he contested with his professors who at that time were used to giving lectures and having their students agree with them without question. He was also having conversations with his classmates about religion. They were members of other faiths, not Universalists. Toribio believed that the only way to learn is by listening, by asking questions, by thinking for yourself, by debating.

It was important to him to have a high school diploma, so he left the farm and went alone to Calatrava in Negros Occidental, coming home every weekend. He took the last two years of high school there at Calatrava

Public High School. The Universalist Service Committee supported him there, not only with money but with encouragement. It was 1960 when he finished his high school education, having already studied at Silliman University. It was then that he moved his whole family to Dumaguete City, and there he continued his studies full time at Foundation University. He was forty eight years old in 1965 when he received a Bachelor of Science in Education from that school. You can see how important education was to him!

The house that the family rented in Dumaguete City was a big house with bamboo floors. It had more rooms than the family needed, so Toribio Quimada rented some of the space to students. There were four of them there at any one time, pupils in high school or college. On Wednesday evenings there was always a Prayer Meeting at which the students were asked to pray, to read something from the Bible, and to say something about it. Not all of them liked to do this, but some of them really enjoyed it. It sharpened their wits and helped them think. Very often a religious discussion occurred between the Reverend Quimada and the students. It was always a real discussion, not just a time when the students were only parroting what they were expected to say.

Toribio Quimada told them, "Support your arguments with reason. Don't just keep quiet."

Education, real education, presents the opportunity to discover new ideas, to ask questions about them and to argue and debate, and then to decide for oneself what to accept and what to reject. This is what Toribio Quimada wanted more education for.

Activity I: A dramatization of the Wednesday evening prayer meeting.

Set the scene. Ask the children what they think prayer is. After hearing their ideas present prayer as a deep and heartfelt wish that will help others or themselves. Make it clear that some people pray to God, and others do not. Prayer does not ask for material things like good marks in Math. For example: they might pray or wish that children all over the world might get shots to keep them from coming down with whooping cough, or that the next time they are teased about being Unitarian Universalists they have the courage to say, "I like being a Unitarian Universalist. We care about everybody, no matter what their religion." Ask them what they wish, or pray for. Respect all responses. Do not insist that everyone participate.

Be prepared for someone who says that prayer does not always guarantee good results! Stress the individual's responsibility in making good things happen. Support for UNICEF can make whooping cough vaccines possible. On the other hand, courage to be a Unitarian Universalist comes from within oneself.

Read the verse in the New Testament from Paul's letter to the Colossians, chapter three: verse 13. This is sure to elicit a variety of responses:

"Forgive each other as soon as the quarrel begins."

You might also quote Paul's letter to the Ephesians, chapter four: verse 31.

"Never call each other names . . . never have a grudge against others."

With the children seated as if at the prayer meeting, discuss with them the Bible passage or passages. Questions:

Does this mean you have to agree with everyone?

How does calling someone a name hurt that person?

How does calling someone a name hurt you?

How do you make up a quarrel?

Do you have to be best friends with the person with whom you quarreled?

How does holding a grudge get in the way of friendships?

Etc.

Activity II: Pictures of what they've learned through education

Say something like . . . the students at the prayer meetings were all going to school. So are you. Think of something you've learned there. Make a picture of it that you can share when we have our closing circle.

Closing circle:

Light the chalice. Invite the children to show and talk about their pictures. Encourage but do not insist that everyone participate. Remark on the importance of education, perhaps repeating the line from the story that goes, "Education, real education, presents the opportunity to discover new ideas, to ask questions about them and to argue and debate, and then to decide for oneself what to accept and what to reject."
Sing the second verse of "Maglipay Universalist."
Choose one child to extinguish the chalice.

Session 7: Wider Horizons

Focus:

Self-esteem

What you will need:

• Words to the second verse of "Maglipay Universalist" printed on a flip chart or chalk board
• Good quality drawing paper, at least 20 x 20 cm (9" x 12")
• Crayons that include gold and silver

As the children arrive:

Have the globe and/or world map available for the children to use. Locate the Visayans, Mindanao, and Nagbinlod. Invite the children to browse among the pictures and books about the Philippine Islands.

To introduce the story:

Say something like . . . being a Unitarian Universalist isn't always easy, no matter where you live. Toribio Quimada certainly found this true about being a Universalist in the Philippines. There was one international religious group that welcomed him gladly and also gave him an award. This is the story of that event, and also of his sad death.

The story: "Wider Horizons"

"We will name this piece of land the Universalist Church of the Philippines." Toribio Quimada had graduated from Foundation University in 1966 and was moving his whole family to Nagbinlod, Santa Catalina, Negros Oriental. What a lot of packing up there was to do. If you have ever moved from one house or apartment to another you can imagine what it was like! Not only were there personal belongings to move—clothes, dishes, furniture, books—there were all those things that belonged to the church—more books, the sound system, the typewriter, the cabinets. Lots and lots of boxes were needed, and lots of help, too. Nothing was to be left behind. What would you be sure to take with you if you moved? (Pause for responses from the children.)

The Reverend Quimada kept talking about Universalism every chance that came his way. Back in 1964 he had listened to a radio program called "Sounds of the Night." On it an anchorman and a small group of people discussed universal salvation: the Universalist concept. Some listeners were for it and some were against it. Those who were against it somehow couldn't imagine everyone being treated equally. Some would surely roast in hell forever! A letter came to the anchorwomen asking that the real minister of that faith come forward and defend his ideas. You can tell by the letter that the person who wrote it was against Universalism, for he said:

"Invite the real minister of that faith to defend his position. Why do you allow such kind of faith discussions on our radio station? Are there no radio regulations (that do not allow other religious ideas to be on the air)?"

The letter was sent to Toribio Quimada. He answered it, but it was a week before it was read on the radio. Those in charge of the station had to decide whether to use it or not. They finally said yes! Lots of letters came in to the station after that from the Visayans and Mindanao, letters from people who spoke against the Reverend Quimada's ideas. It has never been easy to be a Unitarian Universalist. Maybe you've had people tell you that your ideas about religion are wrong.

In Nagbinlod where the Reverend Quimada and his family had moved there were many sugar plantations. There Toribio not only preached about Universalism but he put his faith into action, a very important idea in our religion. It is not only what you say you believe, it is what you do about it. You can say you believe in Universalism's impartialism but if you refuse to play with someone whose religion or skin color or clothes are different from yours, then what you say doesn't mean very much. Who wouldn't you play with? (Pause for responses.)

Toribio discovered that the land where the sugar cane was grown had been gobbled up, bought, by just a very few people with lots of money, even though the peasants who worked in the sugar cane fields inherited from their ancestors were the real owners. They were too poor to pay to have the land made theirs. They were also often cheated in their pay, and often they weren't paid on time.

As you can imagine, Toribio was on the side of the poor peasants, not the sugar cane plantation owners. He became someone that the owners and others in power had to "watch out" for, for he spoke out against exploitation and injustice. (Do you know what exploitation means?) People came to him with their problems when they needed help or guidance. Rebecca, who had been his bag carrier through the jungle, was the typist and sent off the letters to the city and government officials that he dictated about injustice. It was a busy life in Nagbinlod, preaching Universalism and putting its beliefs into action.

Visitors came to see the Reverend Quimada from the UUA—the Unitarian Universalist Association, and IARF—the International Association for Religious Freedom. The IARF is made up of groups of people all over the world who believe we should be allowed to choose what religion to belong to. All the groups in one country are called a chapter. There is a chapter in the Philippines, one in Canada, and one in the United States. Perhaps you know people who have been to an IARF Conference. In 1984 when the IARF met in Japan Toribio Quimada was honored with the Albert Schweitzer Award for Distinguished Service. This award is given at every IARF conference to someone who has really helped people. The IARF meets every three years.

This association helps the Unitarian Universalist Church of the Philippines start projects such as fishing and farming which bring income directly to the people. It supports the high school scholarship program which educates the future leaders of Unitarian Universalism.

It was in 1988 that Toribio Quimada died in a really horrible way. His home was set on fire and he was shot, dying in the flames. His wife and granddaughter escaped by jumping out a window and running to a neighbor's house but Toribio did not want to leave all the things in his office that belonged to the church he loved so much. He said, "I will die with the church materials. My soul (does) not have peace if I save my life and lose those church books and records." Sadly, all was lost in the fire, although a downpour kept it from spreading.

No one knows for sure who all the attackers were. Toribio Quimada helped poor people. He had visitors from the UUA and the IARF. Perhaps some people thought he was against the government. Perhaps some people didn't understand why he had visitors from far away places who believed in impartialism and freedom of religion. All is quiet now on the island, but the investigation is still going on.

In 1985 the Universalist Church of the Philippines
became the Unitarian Universalist Church of the Philippines, part of the Unitarian Universalist Association.
Its founder, Toribio Quimada, is remembered as a kind,
gentle, and peace loving man who was committed to Universalism and cared deeply about justice. The Universalists in the Philippines honored and respected him.
Every year when the Unitarian Universalist Church of
the Philippines has a big meeting which brings together
people from all the Universalist churches in the islands there is a short but special celebration in Toribio
Quimada's honor.

Activity: An exercise in self-esteem

Talk with the children about Toribio Quimada's Albert
Schweitzer award. Who was Albert Schweitzer and what
did he do? What did Toribio do that caused the IARF to
honor him? Ask the children to think about what they do
that makes them special. Have them close their eyes and
listen to the following poem. It may help them think about
what is special about themselves.
What is special about you?
Look for it now.
Don't pretend it is not there.
Think now . . . and feel now . . .
What is special about you?
Is it your smile, your friendliness?
Perhaps it is your voice raised in song
. . . or the way you say "hello," or "hi."
Are you fleet of foot . . . running like the wind?
Are you strong? . . . Can you swim far?
Are your fingers nimble . . . playing the piano or
guitar?
Are you a good listener, or good helper?
Do you excel in math, in reading, in spelling?
Are you an artist, drawing and painting pictures?
Can you hit a baseball into the outfield?
Do you know the names of birds and flowers?

Are you a good cook . . . a good actor . . . a good
writer?
What is special . . . about you?
Look for it now.
Don't pretend it is not there.
Think now . . . and feel now . . .
What is special about you?

After a few moments of silence, just a minute or two,
ask the children to open their eyes. Invite those who wish
to share what they have decided is something special
about themselves. Do not insist that everyone participate.

Direct the children to the drawing paper and crayons.
Ask them to print whatever they have decided is special
about themselves at the top of the paper. Invite them to
make a picture of themselves engaged in that activity. Remind them to be sure to put their names on. If someone
says, "There's nothing special about me," be sure you say
what you think is special. Invite the children to share their
pictures and tell others what is special about themselves.

Closing circle:

Light the chalice.

Engage the children in a brief conversation about
what it was that caused the IARF to give Toribio Quimada
the Albert Schweitzer award.

Sing the second verse of "Maglipay Universalist."

Choose someone to extinguish the chalice.

Session 8: Preparing for the Fiesta

Focus:

A review of Toribio Quimada's life and accomplish-
ments

Preparing for the fiesta

What you will need:

- Words to the second verse of "Maglipay Universalist"
  printed on a flip chart or chalk board
- Flip chart

- Wide black felt marker
- Masking tape

As the children arrive:

Have the atlas and/or map and the pictures and picture books of the Philippines available for browsing.

To introduce preparations for the fiesta:

Engage the children in a conversation about what is needed for the fiesta. Say something like . . . a fiesta is a party with special decorations, music, and food. Ours will also be a celebration of Toribio Quimada's life, so we'll want to tell something about him and how he happened to bring Universalism to the Philippines. Our decorations, food, and songs will tell what life is like for the Unitarian Universalists who live there. The fiesta will be next Sunday.

Activity I: Decisions to make about the fiesta

Write on a flip chart the responses of class members to these questions and any others involved in the planning.

- Where will the fiesta be held?
- Whom will we invite?
- How will we invite them?
- What will be the decorations?

Perhaps they will include the cartoon pictures of the story of the firefly and the apes, the pictures of the special attributes of the children, etc.

- What food will we serve? Who will prepare it? This is an opportunity for parent participation.
- What songs will we sing?

Answers to these questions will depend somewhat on the physical layout of your church or fellowship and how announcements are handled.

Activity II: Dramatizing Toribio Quimada's life

Post the responses to the Activity I questions. Write on the flip chart the children's responses to these questions.

- What do you think was the most important thing about Toribio Quimada?
- What did he want more than anything in the world?
- How and when was his dream realized?
- Who, way back in history, was he like?
- How did he discover Universalism?
- How important to the Universalists was the culture of the Philippines?
- How did the Universalist Service Committee help?
- How did Reverend Quimada, his daughter Rebecca, and others travel as they told people about Universalism?
- What did the Reverend Quimada think about education?
- How did the Reverend Quimada die?
- Who is carrying on his dream of a Unitarian Universalist Church of the Philippines?

Suggest that the class members make a play of Toribio Quimada's life, using the responses to the questions.

These are the essential characters:

Toribio Quimada
Hosea Ballou
Magnus Skaptason
Dana Klotzle
Rebecca Quimada Sienes

Other characters will be evident as the drama unfolds. A narrator is needed to provide a smooth and understandable transition from one scene to the next. This can be one of the teachers or an articulate student. As the drama begins the narrator speaks:

"Toribio Quimada brought Universalism to the Philippines in 1952. He was born on April 27, 1917. He was always a questioner, never satisfied to accept the answers given to him by the powerful church to which his family belonged. What he considered important was . . . "

Begin the drama with the responses to question one, spoken by the class member playing the part of Toribio. Continue through the twelve scenes, with the narrator providing the transitions.

Practice the play at least twice, once to decide how it will go and again to firm it up.

Closing circle:

Light the chalice.

Explain briefly that next Sunday we will present the play and have the fiesta.

Sing the second verse of "Maglipay Universalist."

Choose one child to extinguish the chalice.

Session 9: Fiesta!

Focus:

A fiesta for the congregation
A dramatization of Toribio Quimada's life

What you will need:

- Materials for the decorations
- Tissue paper, crepe paper, construction paper
- Scissors, masking tape, stapler, etc.
- The food: Involve members of the congregation in preparing the food, and setting up a buffet table. This can be parents, members of the congregation, both. Encourage the adults to have the children work with them in the food preparation and setting the table. Adults and children can work together in making and putting up the decorations. Some of the food may be brought from home, Biko, for instance.
- A guitar player who can play and teach "Maglipay Universalist," and other well known songs.

As the children arrive:

They can immediately begin to make the decorations, putting them up, setting the buffet table.

Practicing the play and songs:

At a suitable time call the children away from the tasks in which they have been involved. Be sure they know that they will be returning soon. Try to take them to another room from where the fiesta is being held. Practice "Maglipay Universalist" with the guitar player. Let the children know that during the fiesta some of them can go around with him/her singing these and other songs.

Practice the dramatization twice, making any changes in roles that are necessary.

At the close of the rehearsal the class members can return to their other tasks. Be sure they know how you will call them together again for the play.

The presentation:

At the appropriate time, assemble the class again and welcome the guests.

Talk briefly about what the children have been learning. Invite the guests to look at the art projects that the children have made. This can take place following the dramatization, with the children as guides.

Put on the play. Make sure you mention everyone's full name.

Fiesta:

Some children can sing with the guitar player.

Closure:

Everyone sings "Maglipay Universalist."
Notes:
Possible art work to be displayed:

• Imaginary pictures of hell
• Fruits and vegetables found in the market
• Cartoons of the Filipino folk tale
• Embroidery and/or embroidery designs
• Pictures of what class members have learned through education "self esteem" pictures

This particular plan may not fit your circumstances. Be flexible when making the arrangements. For example: The play may be given to another class. The play may be given only to parents. The play may be part of a church service. The display area may be somewhere else than where the fiesta is being held. An invitation to see the children's art work can be made from the pulpit during the service. The fiesta itself should if at all possible be for the whole congregation. The food preparation and the buffet table setting will take lots of help. You might have a small committee of parents and other adults working on this together. They could meet to make their decisions after church some Sunday. Announcement of the fiesta can go in the church newsletter.

Biko Recipe

- 1 kl. glutinous (sweet) rice (or its equivalent in lb.)
- 1/2 kl. brown sugar
- 2 tall cans of coco cream (available in Oriental grocery stores)
- 1 tsp. vanilla
- a dash of salt
- 1 cup water
- raisins (optional)

Steam rice with just enough water and a dash of salt directly on fire and remove when almost done. Set aside. Bring to boil coco cream, water, vanilla and brown sugar until it becomes a little sticky. Slow your fire, and little by little add the steamed rice and mix it until all of the rice is mixed thoroughly to the mixture. Be sure that all of the rice is covered/coated with the mixture. Cover it. Increase your fire and cook for more or less fifteen minutes. For garnishing the plate you may use leaves: banana or other kinds of leaves. Or raisins could be used as garnishing.

In the United States and Canada if you cannot find all the ingredients make a regular rice pudding. But try to find the ingredients first! This pudding is to be made at home by several families and brought to the Fiesta buffet table. Be sure to supply spoons and small dishes!

Rebecca Quimada Sienes

Maglipay Universalist

(BE JOYFUL, UNIVERSALIST)

Philippine Melody
Toribio Quimada
Transcribed by Barbara Back

From Toribio Quimada
Lyricized by Richard Boeke 1989

1. Be Joy-ful, U-ni-ver-sal-ist, Come cel-e-brate our con-ven-tion.
2. So ma-ny ri-gid Bib-li-cists re-strict our God to an-cient days.
3. Hea-ven is U-ni-ver-sal-ist, In-clud-ing mid-dle, rich and poor.

Of-fi-cials, mem-bers all u-nite, Re-joic-ing in de-bate that's free,
Of-ten both priest and Cal-vin-ists Are preach-ing nar-row on-ly ways.
It is not be ing on a list, That o-pens up the di-vine door.

To teach the U-ni-ver-sal light To strength-en church de-moc-ra-cy.
Re-mem-ber U-ni-ver-sal-ist, The sun of God has ma-ny rays.
Lift up your hearts to loving grace, That rea-ches out to ev-ry race.

Chorus

To teach the hope that is for all, Pro-claim the U-ni-ver-sal call.

Repeat Chorus

Sources

Bonner, Raymond. 1987. *Waltzing with a dictator: The Marcoses and the making of American policy.* New York: Times Books.

Commission of Appraisal of the American Unitarian Association. 1936. *Unitarians face a new age.* Boston: AUA.

Cornish, Louis C. 1942. *The Philippines calling.* Philadelphia: Dorrance and Company.

Crossan, John Dominic. 1994. *Jesus: A revolutionary biography.* San Francisco: Harper.

Francia, Luis H., ed. 1993. *Brown river, white ocean: An anthology of twentieth century Philippine literature in English.* New Brunswick, N.J.: Rutgers University Press.

Fukuyama, Francis. 1999. "The great disruption: Human nature and the reconstitution of social order." *Atlantic Monthly* (May 1999).

Ileto, Reynaldo Clemena. 1979. *Pasyon and revolution: Popular movements in the Philippines, 1840–1910.* Quezon City, Philippines: Ateneo de Manila University Press.

Jensen, Tim W. 1999. "From mythos to merger: A brief review of Unitarian and Universalist history." In *Redeeming time: Endowing your church with the power of covenant,* edited by Walter P. Herz. Boston: Skinner House.

Karnow, Stanley. 1989. *In our image: America's empire in the Philippines.* New York: Random House.

Kiester, Jr., Edwin, and Sally Valente Kiester. "Yankee go home and take me with you." *Smithsonian* (May 1999): 41–50.

Klotzle, Dana E. "The Universalist Church of the Philippines." *The Universalist Leader* (September 1956): 190–91.

Pier, Arthur S. 1950. *American apostles to the Philippines.* Boston: Beacon.

Pimentel, Benjamin. "'White man's' forgotten war." *San Francisco Chronicle* (January 31, 1999): 1.

Rosca, Ninotchka. 1992. *Twice blessed:A novel.* New York: Norton.

Schirmer, Daniel B., and Stephen Rosskamm Shalom, eds. 1987. *The Philippines reader: A history of colonialism, neocolonialism, dictatorship, and resistance.* Boston: South End Press.

Schulz, William F. 1992. *Finding time and other delicacies.* Boston: Skinner House.

Schulz, William F. 1993. Letter to Rebecca Sienes.

Sienes, Rebecca. 1994a. An initial research paper about liberalism in the Philippines. Unpublished paper.

Sienes, Rebecca. 1994b. The struggles of Rev. Toribio S. Quimada: Universalist pioneer in the Philippines from 1952–1988. Unpublished paper.

Silliman University. 1994. General catalog. Dumaguete City, Philippines: Silliman University.

Sitoy, Jr., T. Valentino. 1989. *Comity and unity: Ardent aspirations of six decades of Protestantism in the Philippines (1901–1961).* Quezon City, Philippines: National Council of Churches in the Philippines.

Wei, Deborah, and Rachael Kamel, eds. 1998. *Resistance in paradise: Rethinking 100 years of U.S. involvement in the Caribbean and the Pacific.* Philadelphia: American Friends Service Committee (in cooperation with Office of Curriculum Support, School District of Philadelphia).